A COLLECTION OF ESSAYS

BY ELLYN DAVIS

I CARVED THE ANGEL
FROM THE
MARBLE

D1089190

Published by:

Double Portion Publishing, Inc.
1053 Eldridge Loop
Crossville, Tennessee 38571
www.doubleportionpublishing.com

Some of the anecdotal illustrations in this book are true to life and are included with the permission of the persons involved. All other illustrations are composites of real situations, and any resemblance to people living or dead is coincidental.

This book incorporates content originally published in the Elijah Company catalogs and EJournals, Copyright © 1991-2004. Copyright assigned to Home School Marketplace © 2005.

Please note: Information provided in this book is for educational purposes only. It does not constitute professional advice, nor does it guarantee results.

Unless otherwise identified, all Scripture quotations in this publication are taken from the HOLY BIBLE: NEW INTERNATIONAL VERSION® (NIV®) Copyright 1973, 1978, 1984 by International Bible Society, used by permission of Zondervan Publishing House, all rights reserved.

Cover and interior design by Frank McClung, Drawing on the Promises LLC, www.drawingonthepromises.com

Printed in the United States of America

ISBN 0-983309-70-1

FOR RESOURCES, GO TO WWW.HOMECHOOLMARKETPLACE.COM

ACKNOWLEDGEMENTS

MANY, MANY THANKS TO...

...the thousands of home schoolers who have looked to The Elijah Company and Home School Marketplace for many years to help them raise their own children in their own homes. You have refused to accept the prevailing cultural notion that education only happens in institutional settings and discovered for yourselves that a real education consists not just of head knowledge, but also heart and spirit knowledge and that it is built more on relationship than on relaying information.

...my three sons, Seth, James, and Blake who were the unsuspecting "guinea pigs" in my grand experiment of trying to put into practice all of my convictions and beliefs about what real education could be. Thank you for giving me the opportunity to prove that home schooling really works and to see the fruit of my labors lived out through you.

Ellyn Davis

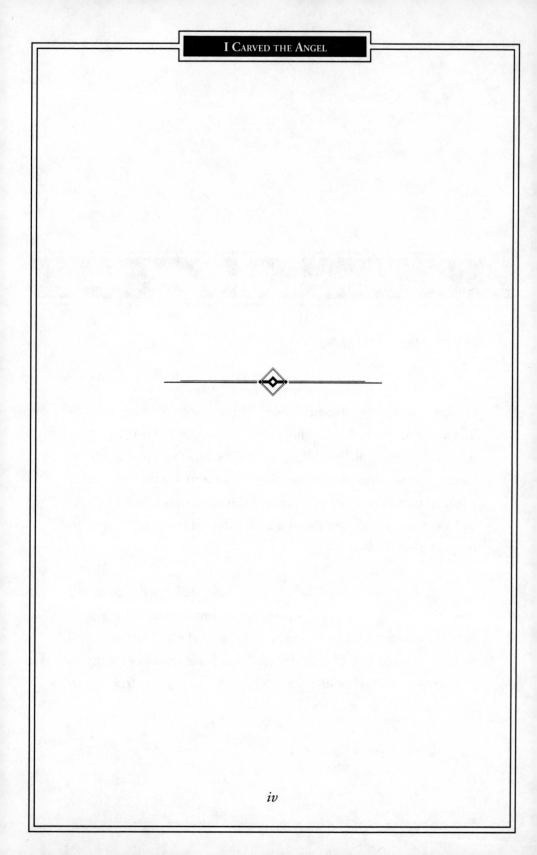

TABLE OF CONTENTS

POSTSCRIPT

INTRODUCTION

THE ARTICLES THAT APPEAR IN THIS BOOK have been written over the course of many years. They represent a journey several of us "old timers" have taken since the early 1980's as we have attempted to raise our own children and reassume the responsibility for every aspect of their lives including their education. The articles first appeared in the Elijah Company catalogs or were sent to the over 20,000 families who subscribed to the Elijah Company or Home School Marketplace e-Newsletters. You may even have seen some of them before as, throughout the years, many have been reprinted in whole or in part online or in other newsletters or periodicals.

People who held on to their old Elijah Company catalogs for years eventually began asking if they could have all of these articles in one place so they would be easier to find, easier to read and easier to make available to friends. So, in 2004, the first compilation of articles was released–*I Saw the Angel in the Marble.* This first book covers the foundational aspects of home schooling–the attitudes, thinking, and environment that allow you to set your children free to become the individuals God created them to be.

The Elijah Company closed several years ago and plans for a second book of articles were put on hold. But, after years of requests from home schooling families all over the world, I finally resurrected the idea of a follow-up book to *I Saw the Angel in the Marble*, and here it is!

I Carved the Angel from the Marble was compiled from articles that focused on the nuts and bolts of schooling at home and the everyday aspects of teaching and learning together. It represents THE BEST OF 15 YEARS OF ELIJAH COMPANY AND HOME SCHOOL MARKETPLACE ARTICLES. You will notice that I am not the only contributor. I've also snuck in a couple of favorites from friends and fellow home schooling pioneers like Deborah Reed, Carole Seid, Valerie Bendt, Marilyn Howshall and Debbie Mason.

In a way, this book took over 20 years to write. So savor it. Read it slowly and carefully. My hope is that it won't just take up space on your bookshelf, but that you will refer to it often and it offers you helpful, practical wisdom and advice.

May the Lord bless you as you raise the next generation!

Ellyn Davis

PART ONE

SETTING THE STAGE
FOR LEARNING

I CARVED THE ANGEL

FROM THE MARBLE

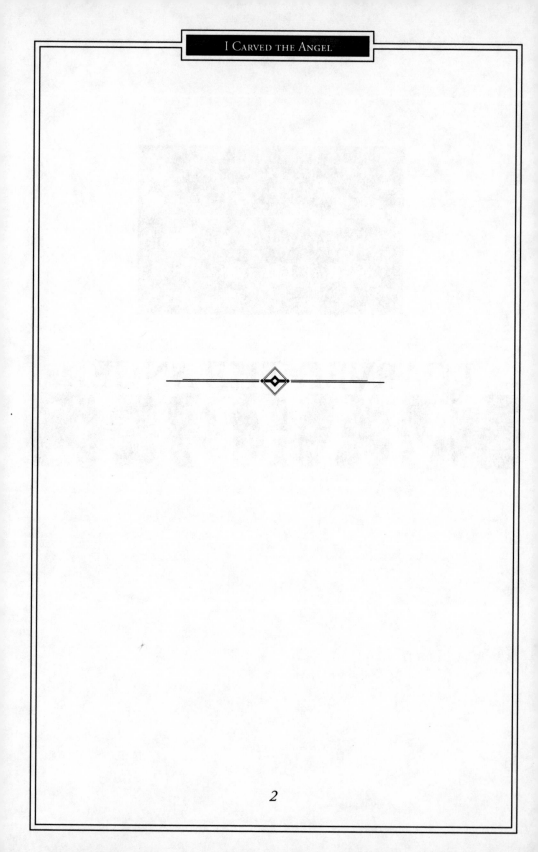

1

SETTING THE ANGEL FREE

IN OUR FIRST BOOK, *I Saw the Angel in the Marble*, we told the story of Michelangelo carving an angel sculpture commissioned by the Pope. One day, the Pope noticed the artist furiously chipping away at the marble and asked why he was chiseling so hurriedly. Michelangelo explained that there was an angel trapped inside wanting to escape and he was trying to release it as quickly as possible.

When the work was complete, Michelangelo exclaimed, "I saw the angel in the marble and carved until I set him free."

What a remarkable statement!

MICHELANGELO'S VISION

There are several things that are fascinating to me about the story of Michelangelo's angel in the marble.

The first, of course, is that the artist was able to see in what appeared to be an average slab of marble what few of the other great artists and sculptors of his day could. The second is that he was able to actually "free" his vision of what the marble could become. And the third is that Michelangelo not only released what he saw in the marble, but he released it in such a way that everyone else could clearly see what he had envisioned it becoming.

So, what does this have to do with home schooling? Actually, everything. Each of our children is, in a way, like Michelangelo's angel. They are like masterpieces hidden within blocks of marble that we get to help "free."

Let me explain what I mean.

A foundational idea in modern schooling is that children are "blank slates," meaning that they are essentially formless and identity-less and like blank tablets to be written upon—empty containers to be filled with all that our culture has decided is "necessary" to ensure they will develop into productive adults.

Another foundational idea is that poorly written slates (slates that have already been "written" upon by unfavorable upbringing, environments, or life experiences) can be "re-written" by the right combination of opportunity and encouragement. All of our government's educational and assistance programs, most charities, modern psychiatry and psychology, and even our penal systems operate from this concept.

NATURE AND NURTURE

The prevailing notion is that people are the way they are because of their circumstances, upbringing and life experiences (because of what has been written on their "blank slates") and in order to change their negative scripts to positive (for example, to help them rise out of poverty) they just need to have their "slates" rewritten. In other words, if disadvantaged people are re-trained and given the right opportunities and resources, they can erase what has previously been written on their "slates" and replace the old writing with new, more useful writing.

In a way, the thinking is sound, because a person's "nurture" can reshape them in profound ways.

All of us know people who have been given that "leg up" out of impossible circumstances and went on to achieve things beyond everyone's wildest dreams, like the abandoned, homeless, illiterate boy in the movie *The Blind Side*. It is the stuff Hollywood films are made of and the reason that one of the great themes in film and literature is the man or woman who was transformed by the right combination of opportunity and encouragement and who succeeded despite seemingly impossible odds.

If you cheered when you first saw *Rocky*, then you know what a strong impact such stories can have on us.

> EVERY CHILD COMES INTO THIS WORLD NOT ONLY WITH A PRESET NATURE AND CULTURAL BIAS, BUT ALSO WITH A FAIRLY COMPLETE SET OF GOD-GIVEN GIFTINGS, TALENTS AND CALLINGS THAT HE OR SHE IS MEANT TO EXPRESS IN SPITE OF THAT NATURE.

But almost every parent knows there is more to the story than "blank slates" which can be written on and rewritten. Our children not only inherit our genes, but they inherit generations of family patterns of thinking and doing and valuing and being—generations of worldviews and "life views." In other words, they come into the world with lots of "stuff" already written on their "slates."

In addition, every family has a unique "flavor," a set of internal guidelines by which it operates, and those guidelines have usually been handed down for generations, just like the color of our eyes or whether our hair is curly or straight.

Our internal guidelines are shaped by our family line as well as by our culture. I know this for a fact because I come from generations of Southerners. The South has its own culture and its own way of thinking and doing things that Southern children are imprinted with before birth.

In fact, studies done on "virtual twins"—unrelated children of the same age who are adopted as infants into the same family—show that even with identical environments, opportunities, and nurturing, those two children invariably have very different personalities.

WHAT DOES THE BIBLE HAVE TO SAY ABOUT "BLANK SLATES?"

From the Bible's point of view, instead of being a "blank slate" or an "empty container," every child is born into this world not only with a preset nature and cultural bias, but also with a fairly complete set of God-given giftings, talents and callings that he or she is meant to express in spite of that nature. And the culture and family lineage a person comes from and the circumstances one faces in his or her life are merely tools God uses to perfect those giftings, talents and callings—the "trials and tribulations" that allow the true measure of who we really are to be exposed and expressed.

The Bible indicates that we are not born identity-less, empty containers. Yes, we are born with certain inherited traits and into backgrounds with predetermined attitudes and beliefs and ways of living life. In other words, we are already born into "blocks of marble" and our upbringing and experiences either further encase us in the stone or help us to free ourselves from it. But, we are also born with an innate, God-given "me-ness." We are individuals who God knew and formed before the foundation of the world and who He predestined to do and become certain things (See Ephesians 2:10; Romans 8: 29 - 30; Ephesians 1: 3 - 4).

Ephesians 2: 10 says that we are God's "workmanship," but that word is often translated "masterpiece." The New Living Bible translates the verse this way: "For we are God's masterpiece. He has created us anew in Christ Jesus, so we can do the good things he planned for us long ago."

SETTING OUR ANGELS FREE

Anyone who has had more than one child understands that children are born with distinct personalities and aptitudes. You can have two children, both from the same parents, both with the same ancestors, both raised in the same environment and given the same nurturing and opportunities, but the two can be dramatically different in temperament, attitude, motivation, talent, innate gifting and level of success in life. We are each as unique as our fingerprints, no matter our background, upbringing, circumstances, or experiences.

So, how do we go about setting our "angels" free from their blocks of marble? I'm not suggesting that we play God. I'm just suggesting that we look at our children differently and act accordingly.

Instead of looking at our children as containers to be filled with everything we plan to pour into them during their home schooling years or as blank slates to be written on, we can totally change our perspective to one of doing our best to discover who each child is and was meant to be and then arranging experiences and circumstances that allow them to manifest all that God created them to become— that "chip away" all that is not truly them and brings out all that is.

Michelangelo chipped away all that was not part of what he saw in the marble and brought out all that was, even using the seeming "imperfections" in his finished masterpiece. It is the same with our own lives and with the lives of our children. God chips away all that is "not us" and helps bring into expression all that is.

But how do we learn to discern the "angel in the marble" in each of our children?

First, we ask for help from the Holy Spirit and from Scripture. We become open to looking at our children as people with unique callings, talents, attributes, and giftings whom God has entrusted to our care for a period of time instead of as obligations or extensions of our own egos or insubordinates we need to bring into "line" or containers to be filled or "slates" we write on. This takes a certain amount of willingness to let go of preconceived notions and cherished ideas of how our children "should" be—a willingness to let go of the "shoulds," and "oughts," and "have tos" and "musts" that were probably programmed into us when we were children.

Second, we take the time to really "see" and know our children. And that does take time, lots of time. Some studies estimate that the average child spends less than 15 minutes of quality time a day with his or her parents. How can we really see and know who our children are and are meant to be if we are spending less than 15 minutes a day connecting to them?

"I *see* you" may be a sentimental line from the movie *Avatar* but it sums up the deep need we all have for what psychologists call "mirroring"—being seen for who we really are, recognized, understood, related to, admired, empathized with, considered special, unique and loveable. Mirroring is one of the primary components in the establishment and confirmation of a child's identity.

Parents are usually selective about what they "see" and value in their children, depending on the parents' own histories, their values, and their desires for how their children will turn out.

All of us have at one time or another felt the pain of not being seen or appreciated for who we are or of having to pretend we were one thing when we are really another. To a child, his or her parents' mirroring not only helps the child see who he/she really is but also confirms his or her identity.

In short, recognizing who each child really is, seeing the "angel in the marble," takes LOVE, real God-like love. The "while we were still sinners Christ died for us" kind of love. It takes the I Corinthians 13 type of love that is patient, kind, does not envy or boast, isn't proud, doesn't dishonor others, is not self-seeking or easily angered, doesn't keep account of wrongs, but always protects, always trusts, always hopes, and always perseveres (I Corinthians 13: 4 – 7).

FIVE THINGS I WANTED FOR MY CHILDREN

When I began home schooling I didn't really know who my children were and I didn't really know what I wanted them to become. So it was a long, interesting process of getting to know them as people, of recognizing the "angel" qualities that were encased in the "marble" of their beings, and of discovering how best to loose and develop those qualities. The only thing I did know was, when it was all said and done and they left my care, I wanted them to have five things:

1. *A deep, meaningful relationship with God.* My husband was a pastor and the P.K. (Pastor's Kid) Syndrome was almost a joke in Christian circles. Many, many children of the pastors and missionaries I knew completely abandoned their faith as young adults. I didn't want that to happen to my children. But I didn't want them to become little "religious" robots either. I wanted them to really, truly know God and have a *real* relationship with Him, with Jesus Christ, and with the Holy Spirit even if that meant they stepped off the beaten path of Christianity.

2. *A deep, meaningful relationship with me.* I also realized that many children reach adulthood with severely strained relationships with their parents. I suspected that a lot of that had to do with the influences and peer pressure they encountered in institutionalized schooling because I had

seen my daughter (who went to public and Christian schools) change from a bright, happy little girl whose mother was the closest relationship in her life to a sullen, rebellious adolescent who considered me a necessary evil.

3. *Work that gave their lives meaning and purpose and that they loved.* In other words, I wanted my children to have "right livelihood." So many of my friends felt like drones in their jobs, trapped doing what they hated because they had responsibilities that wouldn't allow them to risk trying something they would rather do. I wanted my children to think like entrepreneurs. I wanted them to be prepared to support themselves and a family yet still live the lives they truly wanted to live.

4. *A sense of wonder about life.* No disinterested, dead, calloused, hardened attitudes about life for my kids. I wanted them to have what Rachel Carson called "a sense of wonder" about life—an underlying excitement and enthusiasm about the possibilities that life constantly offers us. I wanted them to view their lives as works of art that they, as artists, were constantly co-creating with God. As Rachel Carson described, "A child's world is fresh and new and beautiful, full of wonder and excitement. It is our misfortune that for most of us that clear-eyed vision, that true instinct for what is beautiful and awe-inspiring, is dimmed and even lost before we reach adulthood." I wanted to nourish the delight, surprise and awe one feels when seeing things as a child does for the first time so that sense of wonder would be very much alive throughout my children's lives.

5. *The information and skills to become culturally literate.* I realized that people can be highly educated but still illiterate about what really matters in life. E. D. Hirsch wrote a great book called *Cultural Literacy* and that book summed up the spirit of what I wanted my children

to have—not only facts, but also essential skills that allowed them to navigate life and relationships with relative ease.

This book is an attempt to share with you the nuts and bolts of the process we used to set our "angels" free. To fully understand the philosophy, attitudes, and environment in which we followed this process, it would be worthwhile for you to read our first book, *I Saw the Angel in the Marble.*

This chapter was written by Ellyn Davis and excerpted from the e-book **Seeing the Angel in the Marble** *which contains a more in-depth explanation of how we can "see" our "angels in the marble" and set them free. It is available at www.homeschoolmarketplace.com.*

2

THERE IS A REMARKABLE STORY in the Bible in I Samuel 16. In those days, Samuel was a priest and prophet in Israel. God told Samuel to go to Bethlehem to the house of a man named Jesse because the Lord wanted Samuel to anoint one of Jesse's sons as the new king of Israel. When Samuel arrived, Jesse presented seven of his sons, but he left David, the eighth and youngest, in the fields tending the sheep.

Whenever I've read that story, I've wondered why Jesse failed to include David. Having a prophet of God tell you that one of your sons will be anointed king would be every father's dream. You'd think Jesse would have been elated and would have gathered every single one of his boys together. But he didn't. Samuel even had to ask, "Are all your sons here?" before Jesse sent for David.

If you knew that one of your sons were going to be chosen as king, wouldn't you have had all of them present? How is it that such an honor was going to be given to this household and David was entirely overlooked? The only conclusion can be that Jesse didn't see David the way God did. He was not aware of the greatness in his own son—the son who would actually become his future king! He had no idea *who* was living in his house!

There's a lesson in this story. Have we really looked at our children through the eyes of God and seen the potential God has put in them? Could it be that they are a treasure that heaven has been waiting to release in the world and we just see them as ordinary kids? It is so easy to overlook the ones that we love in our day-to-day busyness and fail to see who they really are. It is easy to judge our children by their behavior or character and completely miss seeing who God is preparing them to become. I like to tell children's leaders to not get rid of the troublemakers in their classes....they are probably future leaders!

There are many remarkable stories of children throughout the Bible. Not all of these children were perfect or even seemed "godly." But it was always evident that God saw something about them that others missed. Did any of their families realize *who* was living in their house?

Consider Queen Esther, raised by her cousin. When he adopted her, Mordecai couldn't have known she would eventually become the queen of Persia. He probably thought he was raising a girl in the traditional Jewish manner to become a suitable wife for a man from her own people. We really see evidence of her upbringing and courage in her willingness to follow Mordecai's advice and, after she became queen, her willingness to risk her life for her faith and her people. This all turned out well for everyone (except Haman) but not because Mordecai understood the young lady who was living in his house. He just raised her in ways he knew were right for a young Jewish woman.

Another interesting child in the Bible is Samuel. His mother, Hannah was barren and prayed for years for a child, promising God that if He blessed her with a son, that boy would be given to the priest to be trained as a Nazarite. It would be an incredible sacrifice for her to give her long-awaited son to the "temple" so to speak, but she was faithful to her promise to God. Samuel was probably with her for the first few years, being prepared for his life with Eli.

The problem with this beautiful story of sacrifice is that Hannah was giving her son to a man who had done a terrible job parenting his own sons. Eli had sons who were drunkards and womanizers! He had absolutely no control over them and he appeared to be a complete failure as a parent because when God told Eli to restrain his sons' behavior, he failed to obey. But, even as a child, Samuel clearly heard God's voice and he eventually became a prophet to the whole nation of Israel at a time when revelation from God was rare.

This Bible story makes me wonder too. Why would God have placed one of His greatest prophets in the care of a terrible parent?

**IT IS SO EASY TO OVERLOOK THE ONES THAT
WE LOVE IN OUR DAY-TO-DAY BUSYNESS
AND FAIL TO SEE WHO THEY REALLY ARE.**

The answer is that God makes up to His chosen ones for any failures of those who raise them. Even though the parents or guardians may not recognize who is living in their house, God does, and works through them anyway.

In the New Testament, we find the story of Mary, who was probably 14 or 15 years old and engaged to be married when she discovered she was pregnant. This situation wouldn't be given a second thought nowadays, but, in her culture, to be pregnant and unmarried was not only extremely shaming but could cost her life. If her husband-to-be chose, he could have ended the betrothal or had her stoned to death. Her interaction with the angel announcing her pregnancy and later as a mother to Jesus shows us a lot about her character.

When an angel confronts Mary, even though it tells her to not be afraid, she begins to argue with the news. "You will have a child," is met with…."I don't think so…" (Paraphrased)! What kind of confidence would it take to argue with a heavenly being? Once the news sinks in, however, her response is astounding. It changes from "Let it be unto me according to your word, " (Luke 1:38) to "….for the mighty One has done great things for me, holy is his name."(Luke 1:49) I don't know how much time passed between the announcement and her ability to begin to praise God, but I believe that any one of us in that same situation might have taken quite some time to say, "Thanks God!"

Mary's response shows us a lot about what she believed. Every Jewish family lived with the hope that their daughter would become the woman who would bear the messiah. When Mary is told that she's the one, she doesn't respond with what might be a natural fear (faced with the consequences of being unmarried and pregnant), but instead begins to praise God! Given her age, this is extraordinary! She must have truly believed the promise that one day a virgin would bear the Son of God. For her to embrace this meant she had great faith. It says more about the way she was raised than just her ability to do the right thing. She had been trained so well in very important aspects of the Jewish faith that when an angel appeared telling her she was to be the mother of the Christ, her response was acceptance and praise. She must have given some thought to her reputation, to Joseph, to her parents, to her friends, and to her community, but she believed the Word of God. A child like this has great faith, which would indicate her family was very serious about teaching her God's promises.

Of course, we know that Mary eventually gave birth to Jesus. Can you imagine being His mother? He didn't need to be "raised in the way that He should go…" but His parents would need to train Him in the scriptures and understanding of the basics of being a well-behaved child. How do you teach a perfect person even though he is still quite human? I could imagine many humorous scenarios. "Who broke this vase?" Mary might demand, only to have the other kids say "Jesus did it! We saw Him!!" But her response was probably more like: "No kids, it wasn't Jesus. He's walking on water in the bath tub right now." I can't even imagine the kind of child Jesus was. I only know that it is very likely that Mary and Joseph didn't really know *who* was living in their house! But God trusted them to prepare Jesus for His future as a son in their family. He was a son with a destiny Who would affect every generation after Him.

At this point you are probably thinking, "Wait a minute. These are all "godly" children, chosen by God for a special destiny. There are no holy, perfect children in my house!" You will be relieved to know that the Bible also has examples of "unholy" kids.

Jacob is a great example. He was known from the beginning as a "heel-grabber" and had a reputation for being deceitful and greedy. I can imagine there were times when even his parents would quite willingly not "claim" him as their son. But even with his reputation and poor character, what did God see when He looked at Jacob? God called him "Israel" and Jacob would be transformed by the identity that the Lord gave him. It would take some wrestling with God's purpose and a vision of heavenly places, but Jacob eventually became who God intended him to be and is known as a father in Israel included in the famous trio: Abraham, Isaac and Jacob. This was God's intention for him all along in spite of his poor character and unscrupulous behavior. Jacob's parents probably would have been astonished by *who* was living in their house.

Another example of an "unholy" child is the boy Joseph. We can definitely see a problem with favoritism from his father that contributed to family tensions. But there is evidence that his own ego kept things stirred up between him and his brothers. His boasting about his dreams only intensified the animosity that had already been created by his father's favoritism. Yes, that's right. The brothers would be bowing down to him! Oblivious to their anger, he continued to explain that his father would be bowing as well. Hey Joe, couldn't you just journal about your dreams? He finally made his brothers so jealous that they decided to kill him! Fortunately, one brother had pity on him and spared his life.

At this point, I am delighted to inform parents that if your children aren't actually trying to kill each other, they are probably doing well!

Joseph certainly didn't have the character we expect of a "chosen one," but God knew who he was going to become and used his circumstances to train him for his future. Ultimately Joseph was responsible for saving and prospering his entire family, the fledgling nation of Israel. Whether or not his brothers regretted how they had treated Joseph in his youth, it is probably certain they had no idea who he would become. They had no idea *who* was living in their house.

It is interesting to me to see how many influential children in the Bible weren't actually brought up by their own parents. This should be encouraging to those who are foster or adoptive parents. You may not know whom God has supernaturally placed in your care. You may think you "chose" your foster and adoptive child, but did you really? Maybe God "chose" you to raise that child. Samuel, Esther, Josiah, and Jesus were among the powerful sons and daughters who were given to others to parent. Knowing this can change our thinking about even the most temporary involvement we may have in a child's life.

The Bible has many examples of children who were not raised by their own parents and even raised in "heathen" ways. Moses was raised in an Egyptian palace. You might assume that a great leader of Israel would need to have been trained by his own people! Under distressing circumstances, he was put into God's hands as an infant with his family not knowing the outcome. Even though there were

17

many things Moses could have learned about being an Israelite if he had been raised by his natural parents, God allowed him to be trained and educated by Egyptians, Israel's oppressors.

All of these children in the Bible had a destiny to fulfill. All of them affected their worlds. Parents or others, who may or may not have seen the greatness in them, raised these children. Many of these children were responsible for saving the lives of their own parents and sometimes even an entire nation.

The truth is that the people who raised them were as significant as the children themselves. I began to realize that the scripture that says "But you are a chosen generation, a royal priesthood, an holy nation, a peculiar people; that you should show forth the praises of him who has called you out of darkness into his marvelous light" (1 Peter 2:9), could just as accurately refer to the parents as to the children we usually apply that verse to. Without understanding the incredible privilege we have been given to direct the paths of our little ones, we can only guess about many of our decisions. However, when we have the confidence that we are co-laboring with God for their future, we get a sobering and delightful glimpse of the mission that is before us.

If we ask ourselves the question, "Who's living in MY house?" will it cause us to make different decisions concerning our children than we are making today? If we let the Lord begin to reveal their strengths, weaknesses, and destiny to us, wouldn't that help us make better choices about how we raise them?

I have rarely met any parents who, despite failure and shortcomings, didn't do their best for their children. It is more obvious to me than ever that once we have done all we can and given our best efforts, God does what we cannot do. We co-labor with Him for our kids.

I have three children and I understand the difficulties that parenting can present. I was young with my first two, and my own insecurities robbed them of the attention they needed to feel affirmed and loved. Twelve years after my second child was born, I had a premature daughter born at 26 weeks (full term is 40). She weighed just over two pounds. As an older mother and someone who had tried to have another child for many years, I looked at this daughter very differently than I had my first two. Each day with her was a gift. I considered her a child who was saved for a destiny and I raised her with that perspective. My qualifications to be her mother were no different than they had been with my first two children, I just looked at her differently. I was not perfect. She is grown now and she's not perfect either. But

---

WE HAVE BEEN GIVEN THE PRIVILEGE OF RAISING SONS AND DAUGHTERS OF THE MOST HIGH KING. IF WE BELIEVE THIS, WE WILL LOOK AT THEIR LIVES THROUGH THEIR DESTINY AND SEE THEM THROUGH GOD'S EYES.

---

she is an amazing young woman who is prepared to affect her world.

Several years ago I realized that when a king has a son, from the day of his birth that child is trained for one purpose—to become a king. There will be things he is taught from infancy that other people are not taught. A two-year-old will be given a little wooden sword. His toy? Maybe, but this child will lead armies and conquer nations. Every part of his life will be guided toward assuming his position of royalty and leadership. There are also some things that he will never do, not because he is being deprived of experiences, but so he will be prepared to lead. We sometimes think that a prince's life is full of indulgences, but a wise king will make sure that his son's every lesson is for the purpose of creating a future king.

We have been given the privilege of raising sons and daughters of the most high King. If we believe this, we will look at their lives through their destiny and see them through God's eyes.

It is not too late to turn and look at your own children through God's eyes and see the treasure they are to Him. Repent for overlooking them if you need to, but begin to train up your children with the confidence that God can do with them what you are lacking. *Who's living in your house?*

This chapter was written by Deborah Reed. Deborah homeschooled her daughter as well as taught in a Christian school. She is a well-known children's pastor and leader who has developed a whole series of teaching materials for children's ministries.

3

THERE USED TO BE a column in one of the popular homeschool magazines about a day in the life of a homeschooling family. Each month a different family would journal about what a day in their life was like. Never, ever did any of these families describe anything remotely similar to what a day in my life was like. Their days seemed to be neat and tidy, full of meaningful family bonding times and finished schoolwork and projects. Mine were more a combination of comedy and total chaos—like something out of a *Pinky and the Brain* cartoon.

When my kids were younger, we didn't allow them to watch much TV, but one of their favorite cartoons was called *Pinky and the Brain*. Pinky and Brain were two genetically altered lab mice living in a cage in the Acme Labs research facility. Brain was a genius who was obsessed with world domination and Pinky was incredibly dense. So every night Brain would devise a new plan to take over the world. But each night his plan failed, usually due to Pinky's bumbling.

Each episode ended with the following dialogue:

Pinky: "Gee, Brain, what do you want to do tonight?"
Brain: "Same thing we do every night, Pinky—try to take over the world!"

21

Through the years I've thought a lot about *Pinky and the Brain*. Maybe because my daily plan for world domination (or at least domination of my world) often ended in failure due to somebody's inane bumbling. Maybe because my homeschooling experience resembled the chaos of the cartoon. Maybe because it seemed like my kids sometimes acted like Pinky and sometimes like Brain. Maybe just because I thought the cartoon was incredibly clever and had a lot of zingy one-liners that my boys loved to quote.

My days usually corresponded to a famous Pinky and the Brain scene where Pinky is on the exercise wheel and Brain asks him to help with the current world domination plot. Pinky, who is running as fast as he can on the wheel, replies, "Just a minute, Brain. I think I'm finally getting somewhere!"

That's what my days were like—running on a hamster wheel thinking I was finally getting somewhere. Many homeschool moms have told me their days are like that too.

One mom described her day like the "Bopping Gophers" arcade game where gophers pop up faster and faster and you have to keep "bopping" them in order to win the game.

MY DAY IN THREE PARTS

Here's what a typical schoolday was like for me when I started homeschooling.

Part I: The Beginning

It is Monday morning. I get up, take my shower and get dressed because Alyssa (not her real name), the woman who works in our home business upstairs, will arrive between 8:30 and 9. And to get upstairs she has to come through my kitchen door and usually stops to put her lunch in my refrigerator. Chris is already upstairs in his office, getting things ready for the day. The boys and I are very tired because church ran late last night and, since Chris is a pastor and we only have one car, we are always the last ones to leave. Also, because two of my children have cystic fibrosis, that meant we did over an hour of respiratory therapy after we got home. So none of us got to bed until close to midnight.

And did I mention that the house is a mess?

I walk a continuous circuit from one boy's room to another, making sure they are up and dressed. At the same time, I am darting back and forth to the kitchen, finishing cooking their breakfast.

Just as we are sitting down to eat, Alyssa shows up sobbing. Her ex-husband Johnnie is behind on his child-support and she is afraid her power will be shut off because she doesn't have enough money to pay the bill. I listen to Alyssa while the boys wander in for breakfast. Alyssa eventually finishes telling me her sad story and goes upstairs to work. While she was talking to me the boys finished breakfast and scattered in every direction.

Everything is already running half an hour late, so I gather the boys and start two of them on their respiratory therapy. When therapy is done, I send them all off to do their morning chores while I put the dishes in the sink and look for the day's schoolwork which, of course, is not where it should have been put away on Friday.

The boys are supposed to feed the horses, dogs, and cats and come right back and start on their math. But they've gotten sidetracked at the barn by a copperhead they find coiled up in the hay. After much poking and prodding and general excitement, someone gets the idea to take a shovel and whack off the copperhead's head. When the boys burst back into the kitchen, I am greeted with a very boisterous recounting of the copperhead adventure and a Ziploc baggy containing the hacked remains of a headless snake they want to freeze for later dissection. (I will find this frozen snake a year later when I am cleaning out my freezer.)

For some reason, all of my children could have been ADHD poster kids, so there is never any such thing as just sitting them down at a table, opening the day's lesson in their math books and starting them on a task at which they sit quietly for an hour doing their work. In fact, there is never any such thing as finding the math books, pencils and paper much less finding the boys without spending 10 minutes searching for them.

I have a friend who homeschools all girls. She has a completely different experience. Her school room is orderly, her home is immaculate, and everything runs like clockwork. The girls get up when their alarms go off, get themselves dressed, help with breakfast preparation and cleanup, do their chores, and dive into their schoolwork by 8:30 AM with no prompting or prodding. They spend endless hours watching ABeka videos without ever wiggling or whining or getting into spitball fights. And when school is done for the day they put all their school supplies neatly away.

I can't even imagine such a scenario in my home. It is so alien to my experience that those girls might as well be Martians.

Sometimes I console myself by believing that my kids must have the Edison trait, or the DaVinci factor, or whatever it is that causes quirky kids who make huge messes and don't fit normal guidelines grow up to become genius millionaires like Walt Disney or Bill Gates or Steven Jobs or what's-his-face who started Virgin Atlantic Airlines.

By now it's nearly 10 AM—way past time for school to start. FINALLY, everyone is up and dressed, breakfast has been eaten, therapy and the morning chores have been done, the dead snake is in my freezer, and the boys are seated around the table with paper, pencils, and math books. It should be smooth sailing from here on out, right?

Not so fast.

James suddenly has to go to the bathroom. For all of the boys, going to the bathroom is usually a theatrical production in six acts— Act I, head for the bathroom but become distracted by something and change course; Act II, spend 10 or 15 minutes off-course before realizing you really, really have to go to the bathroom; Act III, go to the bathroom; Act IV, head back to the schoolroom but become distracted by something and change course; Act V, spend 10 or 15 minutes off-course before Mom finds you and sends you back to the school room; Act VI, resume your schoolwork.

Blake can't find his cat and he wants the cat to be in the room with him while he does his math, so, when I'm tracking James down, Blake runs outside to find the cat. Actually, the cat is only half Blake's because the cat originally belonged to James until the two of them worked out a deal that involved trading Blake's Snake Eyes G.I. Joe for half of James' cat. I don't ask which half of Fluffy each boy owns. I don't really want to know. But it does raise interesting questions about how they will settle the issue when each of them wants to take their half of the cat with them to college—*if* the cat makes it that long and *if* James and Blake ever graduate from homeschool.

Seth realizes this is his opportunity to sneak away, so he disappears into the computer room. When James and Blake get back, Seth has to be dragged away from the computer. He's working on a program he's designing and has just gotten in the groove and doesn't want his train of thought to be interrupted by something as mundane as math. As the four of us march back to the dining room table where math is waiting, someone knocks a potted plant over and makes a mess that has to be cleaned up before it stains the rug. And did I mention that some animal has pooed on the porch? I am alerted to that fact by mysterious, brown, stinky footprints across the kitchen floor. So I deploy a cleaning crew to tackle poo containment before a trail of stinky tracks winds its way through the rest of the house.

As I gather everyone together for the umpteenth time and herd them toward their schoolwork, I am reminded of the phrase "herding cats." That perfectly describes what it is like to round up a houseful of boys and get them all in one place at one time ready to focus on math. I comfort myself with the knowledge that Einstein flunked math as a kid, so maybe there is hope for my boys.

The dog slipped in when Blake came back with the cat and she makes a sudden appearance, starts chasing the cat, and before I can stop them, everyone under 10 (which is everyone but me) is having a great time running through the house trying to catch the cat and dog. It takes until 10:45 before the dog and cat are outside, the boys are quiet and seated at the table and everyone at least has their book and pencil and paper in hand and is showing some indication that they might possibly settle down and get to their math. But, after all their exertion, they want something to drink. That takes another 10 minutes.

Part II: The Middle

Finally, we are actually doing "school." For 30 minutes all runs smoothly. The math books are actually open. Pencils are actually scribbling math problems on paper. I have high hopes that perhaps some knowledge of math is actually seeping into their brains. I savor the moment, knowing it is probably too good to last. Sure enough, soon there is the sound of a truck driving down the driveway. There is immediate pandemonium as everyone starts chanting, "U.P.S.! U.P.S.!,U.P.S.!" Math is forgotten as a tableful of boys drop their schoolwork and make a mad dash to the door to find out if Danny, the U.P.S. driver, delivered anything interesting.

Chris comes downstairs to find out why there is so much commotion. He has fantasies of happy, studious boys sitting around the table eagerly polishing off five subjects by 11 in the morning with the help of their awesomely together mother who not only keeps a tidy, well-organized house but also bakes all her own bread and serves up tasty, nutritious three-course meals each evening even though she ministers at prisons and homeless centers several nights a week. He doesn't seem to realize that he is delusional. Either that, or he's fantasizing about someone else's wife and kids—not his own. He can't fathom how easily the day can just run away from me (and neither can I) because as soon as he shows up the boys jump into their seats and start working furiously at their math looking like angelic future Nobel Prize winners.

Chris returns to his office, but comes back downstairs a few minutes later to run an errand in town. As he is headed toward the garage, Blake jumps up and runs out the door after him to remind him to get more milk. Blake has forgotten that he set his breakfast leftovers outside the screen door on the porch and another of the cats, Rascal, who is in an advanced stage of pregnancy, is eating them. As Blake flings the screen door open screaming, "Dad, wait!!!" the cat is so terrified that right in front of our eyes she rolls over shrieking and literally shoots a kitten into the air. The kitten takes a trajectory that propels it several feet across the porch where it skids to a stop and lies there completely stunned, trying to figure out what just happened. We are all just as stunned. Then we break into hysterical laughter as Rascal gets up and calmly resumes eating Blake's leftovers.

After she finishes eating, Rascal notices the kitten and realizes that it is hers. (The following evening she will give birth to two more kittens in a more traditional manner.)

When all the oooing and ahhhing over the new kitten winds down, I get the boys settled again and tackling their schoolwork. But I know it won't be long before they are hungry. And when Alyssa comes downstairs to get her lunch out of the refrigerator and to tell me her

27

unabridged version of what a lowlife Johnnie is, they will want to eat too. We will be lucky if, during the whole morning, we put in an hour of school. And by lunch time I will be exhausted from a morning spent "herding cats" in the form of small boys.

Part III: The End

But I won't be able to rest because I still have a whole afternoon of more school, of chauffeuring the boys to soccer or to dance, art, or piano lessons, and of trying to review a few of the hundreds of books lining my hallway and pouring over into my bedroom. And then there is dinner to prepare, and, after that, therapy. Hopefully I can get the dishwasher loaded and some cleaning up done before I go to bed. But then again, maybe not.

Yes, there are probably a dozen ways I could change this scenario to make things run more smoothly and efficiently, but I'm just too dadgum tired to exert the energy to undertake the changes I need to make.

It's not that I didn't know what to do. I've read all the scheduling and organizing books. I even have a copy of *Getting Organized*. But I need more than organizational skills. I need time and energy to actually put my organizational skills to work on the chaos of my days. It's not just a matter of knowing what to do, it's finding the emotional and physical energy to tackle it. I needed to de-chaos my life—not just of physical chaos, but also of the mental, emotional, and relational "chaos" and "clutter" that drained me of energy and caused me to feel overwhelmed and undersupported.

So over the years I developed what I call "*The Four Rules to Getting off the Wheel*" and I'll share them in the next chapter.

4

IN THE LAST CHAPTER, I shared what a typical day was like when I first began homeschooling my children.

Thankfully, those days didn't last forever. Eventually the children grew older and more settled into a routine and I learned how to better manage things. How did I feel on days like that? Overwhelmed and under-supported. I would catch myself thinking thoughts like:

- This isn't fun anymore (in fact, it's a real drag).
- My life is spinning out of control.
- There's not enough me to go around.
- I'm trying to keep too many balls up in the air (or spin too many plates).
- I'm drowning.
- I can always just send them to military school.
- Can I run away from home?

I would also have weird feelings in my body—a tightness in my throat, chest or between the shoulder blades; pain in my lower back; headaches or dizziness; chronic fatigue; numbness of certain parts of my body; anxiety and tenseness; difficulty swallowing; nausea; upset stomach or irritable bowel; or ringing in my ears.

OVERWHELMED AND UNDERSUPPORTED

What was wrong with me? I am a highly educated, extremely capable person who has always succeeded in a corporate or educational environment. I should be able to do this with no problem. What was it about running a household and trying to homeschool at the same time that made me feel like a complete failure and reduced me to the level of a blithering idiot? I could manage an office, a laboratory, a classroom of college students or a huge project, so why couldn't I manage a household and three small boys?

Part of the problem had to do with the fact that I had taken on too many jobs all at once.

When I taught in college, the classrooms or offices were already set up and managed by someone else, the curriculum was already chosen for me, there were secretaries and support staff that I could delegate part of my workload to, janitors came in at day's end and cleaned, there was a university cafeteria, there were university buses to take my classes on field trips, and I had no personal stake in whether an individual student passed or failed my classes. All I had to do was get myself to work on time and do my job well in order to be successful.

But this was a different world. Homeschooling was a massive, full-time commitment. Done well, it would require a total reorientation of my life, not just thirty or forty hours of my week. And, I was HUGELY invested in the outcome.

Like it or not, I WAS IT. I was the teacher, principal, secretary, administrative assistant, kitchen staff, janitor, and yes, even the bus driver to take the children on field trips. And when the schooling portion of my day is done, I can't "go home," because... Surprise! I'm already home and my students live with me! I'll still have to make sure they get dinner, help them with their homework, and drive them to their piano and dance lessons or soccer practice. Then I'll have to make sure they have their respiratory therapy done and are ready for bed before I can grab some rest and spend some time with my husband. And I'm not going to get paid a dime for doing all this.

I'm not going to get a lot of appreciation for all I do either. In fact, I will probably be criticized and told I'm some sort of lunatic and that my kids are going to be totally messed up when I'm finished using them as "guinea pigs" for my misguided homeschooling experiment.

Yes, Dad is supportive and encouraging and even helps teach some of the subjects. But I am the primary educator and homemaker. In short, I will be the glue that holds the whole homeschooling, home-life endeavor together.

No wonder I feel undersupported and overwhelmed! And no wonder I feel like Pinky furiously spinning on his wheel and thinking he is getting somewhere!

I needed to de-chaos my life—not just of physical chaos, but also of the mental, emotional, and relational "chaos" and "clutter" that drained me of energy and caused me to feel overwhelmed and undersupported.

It was obvious that I needed to get organized, but more than that I needed to find ways to release the emotional and physical energy necessary for me to face what it would take to get organized. I know all the principles of organization and productivity (in fact, I'd taught them in seminars), but what I needed most was the energy to be able to implement those principles in my life.

What helped me the most? Becoming aware of beliefs and fears that drained my energy and caused me to keep holding on to people, activities, and things long after it was time to move them on their way.

THE FOUR RULES TO GETTING OFF THE WHEEL

Awareness was the first step to being able to let them go. So let me share my *"Four Rules to Getting Off the Hamster Wheel."*

Rule #1: Be "80/20" and "margin" conscious.

In his wonderful books *Margin* and *The Overload Syndrome*, Richard Swenson defines "margin" as the space that exists between people and their personal limits.

He discusses how most of us have squeezed that space out of our lives so that we live chronically overextended lives wishing for

> **IF WE TRY TO CHANGE TOO MANY THINGS ABOUT OUR LIFE AT ONCE, WE JUST HEAP MORE STRESS UPON OURSELVES. AND FACE IT, STARTING TO HOME SCHOOL CAUSES A HUGE CHANGE IN LIFESTYLE AND ROUTINE.**

more time, more energy, more money, and deeper relationships. Margin is the time you need to spend on things that are important to you; the emotional reserves to develop deep, meaningful relationships; the financial reserves to spend on what would enhance your life and your relationships; and the physical health to be able to do what you love to do.

The idea of "margin" blends well with the 80/20 Principle. It is the 80% of people, things, and activities of low value that tends to fill the "space" in our lives and eat up our margin.

Margin is also "space consciousness." We need to clear the clutter in our "inner space" as well as our outer space. Sometimes new and better things and relationships can't come into our lives because there is no space for them. We need to get rid of the old and unproductive that is taking up space in our lives (physically, emotionally, mentally, financially, etc.) to make room for the new. And sometimes we actually need to find more space.

Having too many things in too small a space means one of two things must happen—either we cut down on the number of things we have or we move to a bigger space.

Rule #2: Everything you own, do, or are involved in should have value to you.

What determines value? *First, there is functionality.* Does this possession, relationship, or activity serve a real function in your life? Or is it just another form of physical, mental, emotional, or spiritual clutter? Worse yet, does it drain you of energy?

Some things just make you tired thinking about them. For example, I have a rug scrubber, but it's such a pain in the neck to use that I find myself getting tired each time I think about cranking it up. It's just easier to spot clean the carpet. If you find you have things in your life that are like my rug scrubber, although they are functional, the hassle it takes to use them negates their functionality.

And last month, in a fit of inspiration, I bought several bundles of strawberry plants dreaming of how wonderful it would be to create a raised bed strawberry garden. Reality hit when I got the plants home and thought through what it would take to actually achieve my vision of a bed of ripe, delicious strawberries. The more I thought about it, the more exhausted I felt. So the strawberry plants are going back to the nursery and I'm buying my ripe, delicious strawberries from the farmers' co-op.

Second, there is beauty. Beauty is an expression of God's love so it has the ability to heal, soothe, inspire, and renew. Is this possession, relationship or activity "beautiful" to you in that it soothes, inspires, and renews you physically, mentally, emotionally, or spiritually?

New Agers believe that everything emanates its own spectrum of energy and some things emanate an energy that is draining while other things emanate an energy that is uplifting. I kind of agree with them because I've had the experience of paintings or music or the way a room is decorated just totally turn me off or even make me feel creepy. But I've also had the experience of stepping into a room and feeling suddenly lighter and more cheerful.

For example, I've always loved the look of log homes from the outside, but every log home I ever entered felt claustrophobic and dark to me no matter how beautifully it was decorated. The ceilings always seemed too low because of the dark wood and massive beams and the windows never let in enough light to suit me. When we were looking for our home, the realtor kept suggesting a log home he thought would be perfect for us. But I didn't even want to see it because the inside of log homes always seemed dark and close to me. But the agent persisted until we looked at the house and it turned out that this log home was different. It had high ceilings and large windows all around to let in plenty of light. And the interior dividing walls were finished like a regular, drywalled house and painted to match the off-white chinking between the logs. In other words, the rooms felt spacious and light. We've owned that house for 16 years now.

Third, there is love. Do you really love and enjoy this possession, relationship, or activity?

To determine which possessions have value to you, ask yourself, "If I had to move into a house half as big as the one I live in now, would this be one of the things I would take with me?" That's your baseline for determining an object's worth.

To determine which relationships and activities have value to you, ask yourself, "If I went away for a year, would I want to pick this back up when I returned?" That's your baseline for determining a relationship's or activity's worth.

Rule #3: Focus on one manageable 20% thing at a time.
Multitasking is supposed to help you get more things done quickly, but when you try to do many things at once, everything ends up incomplete. In fact, there are scientific studies that multi-tasking actually is the most ineffective way to approach getting things done. The greatest productivity with the least amount of stress comes from focusing on just one thing at a time.

We had a child with Asperger's Syndrome live with us for awhile and A.S. people are incredibly disrupted by change. So if we wanted to change something in his environment (like rearrange the furniture in the living room) or in his routine, we could change only one thing (like where the couch was), then give him time to adjust to that one change before we made another. Otherwise he would become disortiented.

His resistance to change was extreme, but I think to some extent change is stressful to everyone. So if we try to change too many things about our life at once, we just heap more stress upon ourselves. And face it, starting to home school causes a HUGE change in lifestyle and routine. Ask yourself, "What is the one change I could make now that would have the most impact on what I want my life to eventually be like?" Take baby steps and eventually you will get where you want to go.

Rule #4: Complete significant incompletions.
Anything left unfinished or unresolved becomes a drain on your physical, emotional, mental and spiritual energy. The best way I can explain what incompletions do to you is to tell you the story of a Cocker

Spaniel named Penny we had when I was growing up. Penny had always been very healthy, but suddenly began showing signs of lameness in his hind legs. Within a week, he was paralyzed from the hips down. When we took him to the vet, we discovered that Penny's hind legs were covered with hundreds of tiny seed ticks. One tick wouldn't have sucked enough life out of him to hurt him. Even a few dozen ticks wouldn't. But hundreds did. The vet got rid of the ticks and Penny made a full recovery.

That gruesome story illustrates what incompletions do to us en-

ANYTHING LEFT UNFINISHED OR UNRESOLVED BECOMES A DRAIN ON YOUR PHYSICAL, EMOTIONAL, MENTAL AND SPIRITUAL ENERGY.

ergy-wise. A few incompletions might not seem to matter, but the more we have in our lives and the more significant they are, the more paralyzed our energy becomes.

Life coach Chris Lucerne states, "Incompletions suck the energy right out of you, as they are constantly playing and nagging in the back of your mind every minute, every hour, every day. They are the white noise of mental chatter, the constant barrage of shoulds, the weighty feeling of overwhelm.... And, if that weren't enough, they absolutely stand in the way of you being able to manifest what you want in your life...."

Incompletions come in three categories: (1) Incompletions related to your environment; (2) Incompletions related to other people's behavior; and (3) Incompletions related to yourself.

Incompletions in your environment are those things that are untidy or disorganized or that need to be cleaned, repaired, organized, discarded, redecorated, or dealt with in some way. This includes clutter, stacks of papers to file, taxes to prepare, letters that should have been written, overdue bills, cars that need oil changes or new tires or a brake job, and the thousands of other tasks that we keep putting off getting done. What in your environment (home, auto, office, etc.) causes you to feel irritated or tired when you think about it because you know you need to complete it?

Next are people-related incompletions.

Some people can be "energy vampires" who literally suck the life energy out of us. Maybe they are consistently late, don't follow through on what they tell you so you have to expend energy readjusting your schedule or activities, are negative and disrespectful of you, whine and complain, or constantly spew out stories of their drama all over you.

Or maybe you've had a relational "disconnect" with someone and you need to resolve things between the two of you. You probably already know you need to pull away from energy vampires and sort out relational problems, but keep putting it off and putting up with the energy drain. This "putting it off" is an incompletion that perpetuates relational clutter in your life. I have a friend who had a falling out with a relative over a misunderstanding and every time the family got together my friend would try to avoid that relative. Her son wisely told her, "Mom, even it's not your fault, it only takes 5 minutes to give an apology, but avoiding her will take you a lifetime."

There are several forms of incompletions related to yourself.

1. *Habits*: What do you put up with from yourself? What habits do you wish you could change? What do you do that you know you need to stop doing?

2. *Broken Trust:* I once had someone pray over me who told me, "You have broken trust with yourself." It took me a while to figure out what he meant. Essentially, I had caused me to distrust myself because I had done things that were not in alignment with who I was as a person. Some of the ways I had broken trust with myself were: (1) I had neglected myself and my own needs for the needs of others; (2) I had done things that I didn't approve of myself doing; (3) I had failed to do things I promised myself or someone else I would do; (4) I had pretended to be the kind of person that I wasn't; and (5) I had lied to myself and to others by withholding important information or feelings from them. In other words, the message I had sent to myself over and over was, "You can't trust yourself."

3. *Regrets and Resentments:* Any significant regrets or resentments that you are holding onto keep you a prisoner to the past and drain your energy to live for today. Everyone has regrets for the way they have lived their lives and everyone has been hurt by other people. But holding on to those regrets and resentments just keeps us mired in past pain. We need to learn to let them go—not only to forgive others, but also to forgive ourselves.

Anything not finished in the physical, mental, emotional and spiritual realms clutters your psyche and bogs you down.

Why do we put up with so many incompletions in our lives? I'm not sure, but I have a hunch that we like "open threads." They give us a sense of connection and power. I'll try to explain what I mean.

I had a handyman once named Michael and he liked to leave a lot of what I call "open threads." He would bring a project just to the verge of completion, then start another and leave it undone too. Because he had actually done fine work when he finally completed a project, it put me in the Catch 22 situation of being forced to praise him and pay him for what he had done but being extremely dissatisfied with the job because having it 95% done was a huge inconvenience and aggravation.

For example, he remodeled a bathroom and did a beautiful job on the construction, the laminate flooring, the louvered closet doors, the woodwork, the fixture installation, etc. but he left several pieces of the molding unfinished. The bathroom was completely useable, but every time I went into it, I would see the unfinished molding and paint and it would aggravate me. This went on for months until finally I realized that Michael used the "open threads" to stay connected to me in some way. I'm not exactly sure how it worked for him, but it gave him a sense of some kind of ongoing job security as well as a feeling of power over me.

When I looked deeper, I realized that Michael liked to keep 3 "open threads" going at all times. If there were ever more than three, he would finish something so he could bring the open threads down to his manageable number of 3.

Another reason we like "open threads" is that we actually have a fear of endings. There's something final and depressing about them that makes us second-guess our decision to bring closure. I've noticed that I tend to be able to go gung-ho at a project until it is about 90% finished, then I have a really, really hard time finishing that last 10%. For example, I had been trying for months to get my garage uncluttered and organized. I finally reached a point where I went at it full steam for about a week. I got everything 90% done, then my energy faded and it was like torture to finish the job.

It didn't make any sense, because I was only a few hours away from being done. But what remained was the last, little niggly things that I didn't know what to do with. Should I keep them? Donate them to Goodwill? Toss them? Somehow, having to make those decisions about a stack of things in the corner of the garage became overwhelming, so I stopped and it was months before I could face them again.

I looked around me and realized I do the same thing with everything. My desk is neat except for that stack of papers in the corner that needs to be sorted and filed. My kitchen is orderly except for that one counter. My living room looks pretty good except for that one area that is always cluttered. What's with that? There must be some emotional attachment to incompletion, some residual hoarder in me that makes me stop just short of finishing the job, some aversion to endings and closure. I'm still working on figuring that out.

AND NOW....

Those times when the boys were young and my life was total chaos are in the past. I eventually made my way off the wheel. My house never looked like a decorator showcase and we ate a lot of peanut butter and jelly sandwiches along the way, but in the end, they have each come back and thanked me for taking on the full-time commitment to homeschool them.

This chapter and the one preceeding it were written by Ellyn Davis and excerpted from the e-book **Getting Off the Wheel** *which contains a more comprehensive explanation of how you can "get off the wheel" in your own life. It is available at www.homeschoolmarketplace.com.*

5

LIFESTYLE OF LEARNING is an intriguing expression, one that captures the heart and mind and maybe a little of the imagination as well. It alludes to new ideas, new ways, and freedom!

While the expression "Lifestyle of Learning" does in a way define itself, it is an expression that still requires a more thorough definition. The reason for this is that in our traditional educational system the activity of learning has been distorted from its true nature to look like something one would want to have as little to do with as possible. So, to expect one to want to pursue a lifestyle of it? Not likely. Likewise, the average individual's lifestyle is nearly void of any activity that could be considered a learning experience or educational in nature.

Learning as a lifestyle is not just a nice idea to incorporate into your existing lifestyle or even into your existing educational program in a last-ditch attempt to upgrade or redeem them somehow. Rather, it is truly a change-of-lifestyle issue.

If you were to enter the home of any average family you would find the children (and adults) doing their "thing." These "things" are what make up their lifestyle. Many are found watching too much television, playing video games, hanging around idle, perpetually riding bikes around the neighborhood, and playing with useless toys. A child may bury himself in novels as a means of escape. Children may be antagonizing each other instead of being helpful toward one another. Mom may be little more than a chauffeur in her effort to get her kids to various learning opportunities she thinks are necessary for their education. Indulgence that produces boredom seems to be the rule of the house. All of these "things" reflect the family's lifestyle.

Then what is a lifestyle of learning? A lifestyle of learning is a lifestyle rich in high quality, real life interests and activities that are directed in such a way that they cumulatively will produce an education. It is difficult for us to understand everything that a lifestyle of learning entails because we have preconceived and mixed-up ideas of what education is supposed to look like in our lives, and even what its fruit is supposed to be.

The best way to define "lifestyle of learning" is to define its goals. In this way the hoped-for fruit will also be defined and will in nature be quite different from the fruit of traditional education, even that which is being produced in many homeschools today.

And what produces the differences between traditional education and a lifestyle of learning? Biblical principles for living, learning, and discipling of children.

LIFESTYLE OF LEARNING GOALS

There are three primary goals for a biblical lifestyle of learning:

1. To disciple children to Jesus and prepare them to fulfil God's design for their lives (definable life-purpose).

2. To develop a love of learning in children that will prevail throughout their lives.

3. To equip each child with learning tools from a young age so that the first two goals may be achieved.

Again the three goals are: (1) To disciple the student to Jesus and into a definable life-purpose; (2) To give the student a love of learning; and (3) To equip the student with the learning tools needed to pursue a lifestyle and a lifetime of learning.

These goals may sound simple, but many parents violate the very principles that accomplish them. In addition, the educational system parents often embrace in order to accomplish their goals for home-schooling is designed not to achieve even one goal.

The path by which these godly goals are reached will make the educational process look very, very different from what we are familiar and comfortable with. Our plan must include focused attention

---

LEARNING AS A LIFESTYLE IS NOT JUST A NICE IDEA TO INCORPORATE INTO YOUR EXISTING LIFESTYLE OR EVEN INTO YOUR EXISTING EDUCATIONAL PROGRAM IN A LAST-DITCH ATTEMPT TO UPGRADE OR REDEEM THEM SOMEHOW. RATHER, IT IS TRULY A CHANGE-OF-LIFESTYLE ISSUE.

---

not only on the academia, "school" side of life but even more importantly, focus must be directed toward the lifestyle of the family and each of its members.

Parents must be willing to evaluate their lifestyle starting with how they and their children choose to spend spare time and to acknowledge the truth that these choices are a direct reflection of their character, and thus, a direct reflection of their true education.

With these definitions and goals in mind, let us examine biblical principles that help to shape a lifestyle of learning.

THE BIBLICAL S.A.T.s

The Scholastic Aptitude Test (S.A.T.) is given to senior high students to determine the amount of knowledge they have accumulated during their school years. The test is designed to complement the learning approach commonly used in classrooms. It is also intended to measure a student's individual progress and compare that progress with other students nationwide.

The purpose of the test is to determine if the student is learning what is being presented to him through the school's curriculum, but what the test actually proves is whether or not the student has retained in his memory bank the millions of bits and pieces of information that he has been fed. In other words, the test determines if he has been attending school and if he has a good memory.

The test does not show if the student is being equipped for any definable purpose, if he wants to learn, or if he knows how to learn.

Remember our three lifestyle of learning goals? We might call these goals the science, art, and tools of learning. How can these be tested? By applying what I call the Biblical S.A.T.s. With these S.A.T.s you can evaluate the learning of any subject according to whether the science, art, and tools of that subject have been mastered. These three components are common in all areas of knowledge including the field of learning, the academic subjects, and even the Christian walk.

First, let's explain the three components of biblical S.A.T.s and give some examples.

1. *The SCIENCE of any Subject:* The science includes the theory or general collection of principles, as well as truths and knowledge relative to that subject. It also includes the technical aspects of the subject, and the process principles that make it work. The science has no personality or life of its own. It is simply a system.

2. *The ART of any Subject:* The art includes the skillful practice of the principles pertaining to the subject, and the artful application of the process. The art or activity of the subject should reflect the unique personality, thought process, and conclusions of the one applying the science. The art is the actual heart of the subject where individual expression is demonstrated. It possesses life and passion.

3. *The TOOLS of any Subject:* The tools are the means with which to put the science theory into artful practice. Each subject has its own unique set of tools. Tools help to put a thing together, to create what will be useful or appreciated. When used skillfully, tools will produce a useful product. It is absolutely imperative that the S.A.T.s work interrelatedly in the learning process. If not you will have a sick system.

Example: The S.A.T.s of Cooking

Knowing the concepts of nutrition, how to combine ingredients, and how to plan meals (the science of cooking) does not make a good cook. Many new husbands can attest to the fact that owning a cookbook does not make his bride a good cook. She must learn how to artfully apply the knowledge using the tools specifically designed for each individual task. The one who knows how to cook is going to enjoy cooking more than the one who must mechanically follow a recipe each time she prepares a meal.

Example: The S.A.T.s of the Christian Walk

A parallel example can be seen in how some people approach their Christian walk. Some extract principles from the Word of God and create systems of do's and don'ts. This reduces Christianity to a mere science—a procedure of steps or a system of "have-tos."

Those who do this might have some knowledge of truth, but

without the Holy Spirit breathing life into those truths, are they really true? Without the art, the science is dead: "...for the letter (science) kills but the Spirit (art) gives life" (II Corinthians 3:6).

When the approach is mechanical and functional, a Christian (student) will not enjoy his walk with God nor will the Heavenly Father (Teacher) appreciate mechanical efforts, for "without faith it is impossible to please Him" (Hebrews 11: 6).

Following methodical steps does not require faith. It is all very secure until it doesn't work. Then the system becomes the scapegoat instead of the person who should have listened to God in the first place!

God calls us to "be still and know that I am God" (Psalm 46:10). Attempting to apply biblical principles (science) without the life, understanding, and freedom of the Holy Spirit (art) will simply keep an individual in bondage and produce failure in his Christian walk.

The primary tool God uses to transform us into the image of Jesus Christ is our yielded heart. Without the ongoing heart-search, the Christian has everything but the one thing that represents the Christian faith—a relationship with God.

ELEMENTS OF THE S.A.T.s OF LEARNING

Remember the three primary goals of a Lifestyle of Learning? Those goals are accomplished by using the Biblical S.A.T.s. Elements of the S.A.T.s of Learning that are Unique to a Lifestyle of Learning are:

1. *Science of Learning. LOL Goal #1: Student is Discipled to Jesus and to a Definable Life-Purpose.*

The science of learning is divided into two categories: the process (how) and the product (what). Together these give us the theory or science of learning—one of three components of a quality education.

Educational experts give us many principles, procedures, techniques, and strategies with which to teach our children. However, this focus on the science of learning is often at the expense of the art or heart of learning and the equipping of the student with his own skillful use of learning tools.

The product and the process of learning (science) must be balanced with the art and tools of learning.

Traditional education heavily emphasizes the text/workbook method for the collecting, processing, and communicating of knowledge. Traditional methods stress the product of learning almost to the exclusion of the process. This renders the learning process nearly

---

TRADITIONAL METHODS STRESS THE PRODUCT OF LEARNING ALMOST TO THE EXCLUSION OF THE PROCESS. THIS RENDERS THE LEARNING PROCESS NEARLY LIFELESS BECAUSE THE ART OF LEARNING IS EXCLUDED.

---

lifeless because the art of learning is excluded. When the product is achieved through a text/workbook method the process is dramatically shortened. The goal is to get through content as quickly as possible. Reading a chapter and remembering it long enough to answer the questions or pass a test is an inferior, boring, and lifeless way to learn.

The three-stage learning process may be in operation (collecting, processing, communicating), but without vital life-giving qualities (art) present in the process, we simply have a mechanical system that will not help us reach our goals.

Again, the product and the process of learning (science) must be balanced with the art and tools of learning.

2. *Art of Learning LOL Goal #2: Student develops a Love of Learning*

Remember our cooking example? Common teaching methods are somewhat like letting children read cookbooks and look at cooking tools without ever letting them practice the art or skill of cooking. They get to do everything but learn how to cook.

Without the art of cooking there will be no meals and nothing to eat. Likewise, without knowing how to learn there will be no learning. Are our children actively engaged in the learning process or are they doing the equivalent of watching a television cooking show? This is not exciting for the would-be cook, nor is it exciting for the would-be student.

Just like the cook, a true learner will possess a love of learning. He does not merely read directions and go through the motions, but has varied, creative ways of approaching his task and is able to produce a product that reflects his personality. His developing ability to learn on his own will bring him great joy and a deep sense of accomplishment. "Art" is the very essence of any field. Art will always suggest that human creativity is present in the process.

There is a simple way to determine whether or not the art of learning is actively present in a student's life.

I have discovered seven qualities that must be collectively working that will show the presence of the art of learning. They are what I call the *Seven Natural Vital Signs of the Learning Process* and they are: (1) individual, (2) delight directed, (3) life-related, (4) valuably active, (5) productive, (6) self-motivated, and (7) focused. These life-giving elements must be evident throughout not only the student's individual learning process, but his lifestyle of chosen activity as well. In fact, the best place to begin making changes is in the child's use of his free time.

The vital signs are like little lights that you can hold up over every part of your children's lives (and of your life) to examine and monitor the quality of your lifestyle activities. The vital signs do not typically play a role in the traditional learning process.

3. *Tools of Learning. LOL Goal #3: Student is Equipped with Tools of Learning*

The traditional approach also reflects the absence of the student's command of five learning tools: research, reason, relate, record, and rhetoric. The learning tools can be applied to any field of thought and are adaptable to all learning tasks no matter how the study is pursued. Possessing a good command of these tools helps the student acquire a true education.

In the traditional system the student remains passive, doing little if any real learning. He is not taught how to use the very tools that will equip him for a lifelong adventure in learning.

When a student is truly learning, he actively and consistently embraces an area of interest (science) that will lead him in a process (science) that reflects his individual expression and character development (art). He will apply the learning tools in a variety of informal as well as formal ways.

It is important to remember that the biblical learning process can not be reduced to a mere collection of multiple choice questions for the student to answer in order to prove he is learning. Can an appraisal be made of an individual's Christian walk based upon his possession of biblical knowledge? Instead, an examination of the Christian's chosen activities, his heart condition, and of his character are the means to determine if he is engaged in a vital discipleship process.

The Biblical Science, Art, and Tools of Learning provide a thorough means by which we can evaluate our children's true education.

Rearing godly children who hunger and thirst for a living God will require a living educational process. We need to be aware of the serious educational gap that is created when even one of the lifestyle of learning components is missing from a child's learning process. Once the components are in place, education becomes a matter of quality-control where the parent continually fine-tunes and monitors the learning process.

A NEW SYSTEM

Instead of operating within the traditional age-graded system, I designed a new system that will easily facilitate the meeting of student-delight-directed and parent-directed lifestyle of learning goals.

The Biblical Lifestyle of Learning framework consists of four seasons. Three are derived from the learning stages that pattern a child's growth and development. The three main seasons are: the collecting, processing, and communicating of knowledge. The fourth season is preparing the young child for the other three.

When the science, art, and tools are operating in each season, true learning is present. However, it is important to determine who is doing the collecting, processing, and communicating of knowledge—the student or the teacher. The one who is engaged in the three activities is the one who is learning. If a student is being spoon-fed from someone else's study, he is not really learning.

To replace the text/workbook/lecture approach to teaching, I developed two natural study models for a lifestyle of learning: *The Unit of Life Approach* (for child and parent-directed informal learning from childhood through adolescence) and *The Life Message Approach* (for formal learning from adolescence through adulthood).

Each approach consists of its own unique set of four natural learning models that build on and complete each other. Each approach brings vision and the needed order and goal-setting direction to help us plan our way in a biblical lifestyle of learning approach.

IN CONCLUSION

Let us for a moment consider the problems confronting us as Christian homeschoolers. Our generation was not taught how to learn and was never given a love of learning. Few of us can access the Word of God for ourselves and even fewer know how to access the Lord in an intimate way. Yet our children are trained with the same methods that failed to teach us to learn or to love learning.

With only the raw material of our fragmented lives to work with, we attempt to integrate our new vision, godly desires and goals into our old lifestyles and systems. In so doing, we create an additional problem—burnout! We use the world's methods to try and produce something they were never designed to produce. When we finally accept the truth that the old way will not produce the results we want, we are ready to receive the suggestion of a new way.

That is what Lifestyle of Learning is all about—a new way, a new system, and a fresh beginning for the entire family. My hope is to encourage you with practical solutions to common problems that will propel you into a higher level of understanding about education and a wonderful new homeschool adventure.

I also wish to challenge you to seek God for your homeschool. His burden is easy, His yoke is light.

He said, *"Are you tired? Worn out? Burned out on religion? Come to me. Get away with me and you'll recover your life. I'll show you how to take a real rest. Walk with me and work with me. Watch how I do it. Learn the unforced rhythms of grace. I won't lay anything heavy or ill-fitting on you. Keep company with me and you'll learn to live freely and lightly"* (Matthew 11:28-30, The Message Bible).

6

TRADITIONAL EDUCATION CREATES THE MINDSET of a wage earner, not of a business owner, and the goal of a typical institutional education focuses on developing the skills necessary to become an employee. So schooling usually creates a mindset and a skill-set focused on working for someone else's business.

We think there is a better way. Whether your child takes a job or not, that child should be equipped with the mindset and skill-set to create his or her own business. An entrepreneurial mindset is totally different from a wage-earning mindset, and becoming an entrepreneur requires different skills. Neither of these is usually taught in public schools, and, because home schoolers tend to base their curriculum choices on the public school scope and sequence, entrepreneurship and an entrepreneurial mindset are seldom taught in a home school setting.

There are only six core skills that enable anyone to be able to succeed at whatever they want to do. These six core skills are usually never taught in school, or if they are taught at all, they are reserved for graduate programs in business college.

Parents can help develop these core skills in their children, but it is not going to be easy, because there is no pre-set curriculum to follow. And because, as a parent, you have probably never been taught these skills yourself, it may be difficult to pass them on to your children.

Also, developing these skills can be expensive, and parents, especially home schooling parents, tend to be on the frugal side.

But the best way to develop these skills is through an experience in business, because all six core skills are necessary for success in business.

WHAT ARE THE SIX CORE SKILLS THAT GUARANTEE SUCCESS?

Core Skill #1: Self-understanding. This includes an understanding of innate gifting and capabilities—mental, emotional, physical, and spiritual. A person who understands his or her gifts and abilities can use strengths to their best advantage and find ways to compensate for or work on weaknesses. People with self-understanding also tend to be more decisive because they know what they want and they know which types of situations "fit" them. They know how to bring out the best in themselves.

Core Skill #2: Understanding human nature. This means you know what motivates people, you can predict how they will act in certain situations, and you know how to work with all different types of people.

Core Skill #3: The art of rapport. This has an element of understanding people to it, but is more the ability to connect with people in such a way that they like and trust you and will allow you to influence them.

Core Skill #4: The ability to "network." There is an old saying that, "It's not what you know, it's who you know." A companion to that statement is, "It's not who you know, but who knows you." Many prominent business leaders believe that your network equals your net worth. By that they mean that your ability to create connections with people will determine your financial future and the level of success you will have in any endeavor. So most leaders look for the people who are the critical connections to their success.

Core Skill #5: Understanding the principles of living a successful life. This includes the principles of operating a successful business.

A FAMILY BUSINESS CAN PROVIDE YOUR CHILDREN WITH MYRIAD "SCHOOLING" OPPORTUNITIES AS WELL AS PROVIDE THEM WITH REAL BUSINESS SKILLS THAT THEY CAN PUT TO USE AS ADULTS.

Core Skill #6: Understanding the specific skills needed for the area in which you want to succeed.

HELPING YOUR CHILDREN BECOME ENTREPRENEURS

Entrepreneurship is responsible for many of the jobs in America. In fact, America's small businesses create 75% of the new jobs in the United States.

A study in entrepreneurship need not be a moneymaking venture in order to be a successful experiment for your child. Giving him a chance to analyze a business situation and being responsible for the outcome will go a long way to prepare him for adulthood.

Teaching entrepreneurial skills to children is not a new phenomenon; kids have been setting up lemonade stands and delivering newspapers across the United States for decades. Small ventures such as these teach children a good lesson in the value of money, in understnding consumer habits, and in learning how to deal with the success or failure of working in the real world.

But what if your children were involved in a "real" business? A family business?

A family business can provide your children with myriad "schooling" opportunities as well as provide them with real business skills that they can put to use as adults. Take math, for example. Learning how to balance a budget and arrive at a bottom line will not only test a child's arithmetic abilities, but using a computer spreadsheet and knowing how to read a financial report will arm him with marketable job skills if he decides to enter the workforce instead of operate his own business.

Your older child will never forget the various challenges involved in writing a comprehensive business plan, including the need for effective research and writing skills. A student tasked with finding a consumer need and filling it will have an enhanced knowledge of sociology as well as current events. And interacting with customers is a real education in negotiation and understanding human nature. Children will also learn firsthand how what consumers want changes over time, and therefore, how a market changes. All of this will provide valuable lessons that can be learned early in life.

Many children who "catch" the idea of entrepreneurialism start their own businesses and do well at them. A small-scale business venture conducted under a parent's supervision is a great way to start, because it minimizes the potential for failure.

This chapter was written by Ellyn Davis and excerpted from the e-book **Starting and Building a Family Business** *available at www.homeschoolmarketplace.com.*

7

WHAT DO THEY REALLY NEED TO KNOW?

WHEN YOU WERE IN SCHOOL, you probably had to learn a lot of things that made you throw up your hands and say, "This is stupid! When in the world am I ever going to need to know this?" And you were probably right.

In high school, I took two years of Algebra, one year of Geometry, a year of Trig and a year of Advanced Algebra. When have I ever used all that math? Never! Sometimes I've had to determine the radius of a circle or the hypotenuse of a triangle and sometimes, but very rarely, I have had to figure out a proportion by using x as a variable.

I studied one subject—math—for five years in high school just so I could use it to solve some basic math problems as an adult. And since now we have super-calculators and the internet, I could probably find out what I need to know without using any math at all. But I had to have those math courses to enter a pre-med course of study in college. And it's still a mystery to me why med schools consider algebra and higher math important for doctors to learn.

The real "take-away" value of those math courses was not the math I learned but the fact that algebra, geometry, calculus, and trig force you to think abstractly and broaden your mental capacities for problem solving. Those skills are highly useful, but I now wonder if there might have been a different, more efficient way to have acquired them than spending five years in class doing math problems.

On the other hand, I took three years of Latin, which is a dead language and hardly ever used outside of academic circles. I also took two years of German and a smattering of Greek and French. As, strange as it may seem, Latin and Greek became more useful to me as an adult than algebra, geometry, trig, calculus, German, or French. Why? Because studying those two languages helped me develop an extensive vocabulary as well as taught me the basic structure of language, both of which have served me well in business, in my personal life, and in teaching my children.

If you think about all the things you wanted to do and learn as you were growing up but were kept from doing by adults who believed they knew what you *should* be doing and what you *should* be learning, it makes you wonder what of all they thought you should learn and do has had any real value to you as an adult. Especially since most of what you learned was remembered just long enough to pass a test before it was forgotten because it didn't mean anything to you.

If the 80/20 Principle is really true, then only 20% of what we learned growing up and in school has served us well. The other 80% was a waste of our time and energy. So, as parents, why don't we spend some time figuring out the 20% of what we were taught that wound up being valuable to know and make sure that 20% is taught to our children? In other words, what if that 20% of knowledge we found to be essential could become our core home schooling curriculum?

FINDING THE 20% THAT REALLY MATTERS

Since we wind up never having to use a lot of what we learn in school and its real value has nothing to do with its "course" content, what if we could narrow down what we teach our children to what we have a pretty good idea they are going to need to know in adult life?

Knowing that learning some information may be a waste of time but learning other information actually becomes foundational to what you may find yourself doing as an adult, the trick is to discover which information should be included in your children's course of study. It is worth our time as home educators to take a look at which areas of learning have served us well and which haven't.

IF THE 80/20 PRINCIPLE IS REALLY TRUE, THEN ONLY 20% OF WHAT WE LEARNED GROWING UP AND IN SCHOOL HAS SERVED US WELL. WHAT IF THAT 20% OF KNOWLEDGE WE FOUND TO BE ESSENTIAL COULD BECOME OUR CORE CURRICULUM?

How can we do this? The easiest way is to do the simple exercise below. So let's dive in. Answer the following questions and work through the following activities.

1. **What was I taught that I really needed to know and think my children need to know?** Take out a piece of paper and make three columns. Label the columns "Academics," "Practical Skills," and "Relationships." List as many things in each column you were taught that in the course of your life you have found that you *really* needed to know. And don't just include academics. Include practical skills , relational skills, life skills and anything else you can think of that you've found useful to know.

2. **What do I wish I had been taught that I've discovered that I really needed to know and want my children to learn?** Do this exercise in the same way as #1, except your list is going to be of those things you *weren't* taught that you wish you had been.

3. **What was I taught that I didn't need to know and don't foresee either me or my children ever needing to know?** Do this exercise in the same way as in Questions 1 and 2, except your list is going to be of those things that you found to be a complete waste of time for you to learn.

4. **Knowing what I do about each of my children, what are the adult roles I expect each of them to assume?** Adult life consists of assuming roles in four basic arenas: (1) Public (situations, relationships, and interactions outside of our immediate family), (2) Friends (interactions with close non-family relationships); (3) Family (interactions with those related to us), and (4) Private (our inner spiritual, emotional, and mental life). Each of these arenas has its own set of demands and responsibilities.

5. **What Academics, Practical Skills, and Relationships will they need in order to fulfill those roles?**

RELATIONSHIPS, LIFE SKILLS, INFORMATION

Now that you have your answers to the five questions, you can create a list of the relationships, practical life skills and information that you believe are most important for your children to learn in their home schooling years.

In our family, we took a piece of paper and divided it into 3 columns. At the top of Column 1, we put "Relationships." Column 2 was

"Life Skills," and Column 3 was labeled "Information."

Then we took our answers to the 5 questions and brainstormed the relationships, skills, and information we thought would be important for each of our children to have mastered by the time they left our care. Our major categories were as follows:

Column 1: Relationships

- *With God* (Spiritual habits such as prayer, worship, Bible Study, etc.)

- *With Self* (Healthy self-image, self-control, purity of thought life, proper eating habits, care of body, etc.)

- *With Others* (Social skills, emotional intelligence)

- *With Created Things* (Proper attitude toward and management of time, money, property, animals, work, etc.)

Column 2: Life Skills (Practical Skills)

- Social Skills

- Business Skills

- Money Management

- Land Management

- Household Management

- Time Management

- Organization

- Playing an Instrument

- Basic Art Skills

- Thinking Skills

- Problem-Solving Skills

- Conflict-Resolution Skills

- Decision Making Skills

- Gifting/Aptitude/Interest Skills

Column 3: Information (Academics)

- Reading

- Writing

- Speaking

- Math

- Science

- History

- Foreign Language

- Art

- Music

- Bible

Once we knew the major areas we wanted to cover, in our next brainstorming session we fleshed out each major area in more detail. For example, under "Money Management," we wanted our children to be able to do such things as: balance a checkbook; choose wise investments; start and grow a business; build good credit without getting deep in debt; read a spreadsheet; master basic accounting, understand a financial report, etc.

Your family's priorities may be different than ours, so you may value different types of relationships, life skills, and academic knowledge than we do. Or you may prioritize differently than we do. That's

OK. There are many avenues to competent, creative adulthood and it would be a boring world if everyone were the same.

The point is to have some sort of idea of what constitutes "completion" in your children's education so you have a target to aim toward. Based on your answers to the questions, you can create a chart of Relationships, Life Skills, and Information like the example of the chart we used in our family, except it will be specific to your family.

This chapter was written by Ellyn Davis and excerpted from the e-book **Creating Your Own Course of Study** *available at www.homeschoolmarketplace.com.*

8

NOW IT'S TIME TO GET SPECIFIC about the relationships, life skills, and information you want your children to master before they leave their home schooling years with you. Here's how you can do it in three easy steps.

STEP 1: DETERMINE WHAT YOU THINK AN EDUCATION SHOULD INCLUDE
If you read the last chapter and answered its five questions, you've got a pretty good idea of what you believe is important for your children to know. This doesn't mean you will only teach them what is on your lists because your state's laws and your child's future college requirements are going to mandate certain courses. However, your lists can become the basis of your "core curriculum" for each child.

STEP 2: DO A LITTLE MORE RESEARCH
Our recommendation is that you do the following five things:

1. First, take a long, hard look at the presuppositions and objectives of institutional education by reading books such as John Gatto's and John Holt's. Why? Because, we are so used to thinking of school as children sitting in desks, listening to lectures, and working on pre-packaged curriculum for six hours a day, 180 days a year, over a period of twelve years, that we have a hard time imagining any other way.

Also, many products for home educators are merely repackaged versions of public school materials, and we need to be able to recognize them as such. Otherwise, we unwittingly find ourselves adopting the same scope and sequence, the same methods, and the same standardized curriculum that was derived from the public school's presuppositions and that seeks to achieve its objectives. We will worry if our children aren't reading by the time they are six or doing fractions by nine. We will guide our children toward popular careers. We will feel unqualified to teach without an education degree.

In short, until we understand the misconceptions behind public schooling, we will think that some form of traditional institutionalized education is true education.

For most of us, our public school upbringing has steeped us in ideas about education that have to be discarded if we want to effectively educate our own children at home. As John Gatto says, "School was a lie from the beginning, and it continues to be a lie." If we know no better, we may buy into the lie and perpetuate its thinking.

2. Second, examine the viewpoints and teaching approaches that currently influence home education. You can read about these in chapters 8, 9, and 10 of *I Saw the Angel in the Marble* or in our guide about common teaching approaches and you can read books that more thoroughly explain the different viewpoints and approaches. If there is a particular emphasis or teaching approach that appeals to you, take the time to learn about it. The fact that it appeals to you may be the Lord's gentle nudge in that direction.

3. Third, try and get in touch with your family's convictions and values and the real needs of your children (See Chapters 3 - 7 of *I Saw the Angel in the Marble* and our guides on *Seeing the Angel in the Marble, See How They Grow, Helping Them to Get It*, and *Creating Your Family's Mission Statement* at www.homeschoolmarketplace.com). Once you have an idea of what you really want for your children, you will be better prepared to chart your home schooling course.

4. Fourth, buy several home school resource books that give an overview of home schooling. These books will overwhelm you if you don't already have an idea of where you want to go with home schooling, so don't dig into them until you have some sense of your family's convictions and the real needs of your children.

Start with books such as *Homeschooling the Early Years, ...the Middle Years,* and *...the Teen Years.* They provide general information about teaching each age group. From there begin looking at curriculum guides like Mary Pride's or Cathy Duffey's. Educate yourself about "what's out there."

5. Create your own Scope and Sequence. If you've never heard the term "Scope and Sequence," it is simply a list of the information that should be learned (scope) and the order in which it should be taught (sequence) from preschool through twelfth grade. You can find a typical course of study for elementary and high school ages online at this link:

www.homeschoolmarketplace.com/course_of_study.html

A TYPICAL COURSE OF STUDY

A "typical course of study" covers certain subjects at each grade level as follows:

Subjects by Grade Level

- *Preschool*: Size, Colors and Shapes, Reading Readiness, Numbers, Position and Direction, Time, Listening and Sequencing, Motor Skills, and Social-Emotional Development.

- *Kindergarten:* Social Studies, Science, Language Arts, Health and Safety, and Mathematics.

- *Elementary (Grades 1-5)*: Social Studies, Science, Language Arts (Reading, Handwriting, Composition), Health and Safety, and Mathematics.

- *Middle School/Junior High School (Grades 6-8):* Social Studies, Science, Language Arts, Health and Safety, and Mathematics.

FOR MOST OF US, OUR PUBLIC SCHOOL

UPBRINGING HAS STEEPED US IN IDEAS ABOUT

EDUCATION THAT HAVE TO BE DISCARDED

IF WE WANT TO EFFECTIVELY EDUCATE OUR

OWN CHILDREN AT HOME.

- *High School (Grades 9-12):* Social Studies, Science, Language Arts, and Mathematics (Algebra, Trigonometry, Calculus, Probability and Statistics).

General Subject Categories

- *Social Studies* includes geography, history, government, and sociology (culture and human relations).

- *Science* includes biology, botany, geology, chemistry, physics, astronomy, environmental conservation, psychology, etc.

- *Language Arts* includes letter recognition, phonics, reading, spelling, grammar, writing, composition, research, etc.

- *Health and Safety* includes physical health, mental health, nutrition, fitness, anatomy, disease and illness, accident prevention, first aid, etc.

- *Mathematics* includes basic math, geometry, algebra, trigonometry, calculus, probability and statistics, etc.

You might want to start by looking at the course of study for the grades each of your children would be in if they were in public school. We never really did grade levels with our children, but looking at what they would have been learning if they were in public school was helpful to see if we were leaving any important gaps in their education.

Just take a look at what is usually taught in school, but don't get too overwhelmed. You want to take the good "bits" from a typical public school course of study and incorporate them into your home schooling. But more than that. What you really want to do is build your own course of study for each child.

Once you realize that you're not preparing your children to become cogs in some industrial wheel but to be competent, productive adults, you will be able to look at the "official" scope and sequence in a whole new light. You will be able to prioritize what your children really need to know and you will probably discover that you want them to know more than is on a typical course of study for their age level, not less.

CREATING YOUR OWN COURSE OF STUDY

You can create your own Scope and Sequence by building a course of study for your children around all the things you realize that a person really needs to know, taking into account the educational philosophy that you tend to favor.

A typical course of study can provide a nice list of suggested topics to teach, but once you know the relationships, life skills, and information you want your children to master, you can add or subtract or change the order as you see fit. You're not doing it "wrong" if your child doesn't learn to read until he's 9 or doesn't study magnetism until he's 12. The end result is what matters. And since you've begun with the end in mind, you know the big picture and you can fit the pieces in wherever they fit best.

And you can do it all in such a way that you ignite your children's desire to learn more, you nurture their sense of wonder, you help mold their character and their ability to think for themselves, and you prepare them to have the skills they'll truly need as adults.

One of the best things about doing it that way is you won't ever have to ask yourself, "Have my kids learned what they're supposed to have learned by now?"

This chapter was written by Ellyn Davis and excerpted from the e-book **Creating Your Own Course of Study** *available at www.homeschoolmarketplace.com.*

9

CREATING YOUR OWN SCOPE AND SEQUENCE

BY NOW YOU SHOULD HAVE A GOOD IDEA of the relationships, life skills, and information you feel are important for your children to master.

Now let's start with just one of the children you plan to home school. Let's call her Suzie.

Step 1. Go to www.homeschoolmarketplace.com/course_of_study. html. Find the course of study recommended for Suzie according to her age and the approximate grade level she would be in if she were in public school. Take a look at the general learning requirements for that grade level.

Step 2. Print out that course of study. Let's say that in public school, Suzie would have been assigned to sixth grade. This means her typical course of study would cover these five subjects:

Social studies
Science
Language arts
Health and safety
Mathematics

The course of study lists what is generally taught in sixth grade in each of those subjects and also shows you the sequence in which things are usually taught.

But, because you did the exercises in the previous chapters, you want to add two more broad categories to Suzie's course of study: Relationships and Life Skills.

When you break down the Relationships you want Suzie to master into "subjects" based on the future roles you foresee her playing as an adult, you may discover that Relationships includes Bible Study (relationship with God); Family Involvement (relationship with family), Community Involvement (relationship with community). And you may discover that the Life Skills you want her to master are things like Household Management and Typing and Computer Science and Entrepreneurship.

Also, according to your lists, you may want Suzie to add some fine arts or music to her school year. So now Suzie's sixth grade course of study covers these subjects:

Social studies

Science

Language arts

Health and Safety (which could fall under Relationship with self)

Mathematics

Bible Study (you determine what this encompasses)

Family Involvement (you determine what this encompasses)

Community Involvement (you determine what this encompasses)

Household Management (you determine what this encompasses)

Typing

Basic Computer Knowledge

Basic Entrepreneurship

Fine Arts (could be drawing, painting, ceramics, dance, etc.)

Music (could be a course in studying great composers or could be music lessons)

Step 3. Based on the typical course of study for sixth grade, you already know what Suzie is expected to cover in Social Studies, Science, Language Arts, Health and Safety, and Mathematics.

Now what you have to determine is, according to Suzie's level of physical, emotional, intellectual, and spiritual maturity, what are the other subjects going to cover? If you are unsure if the relationships, life skills, and information on your lists are physically, emotionally, intellectually and spiritually developmentally appropriate for Suzie, you can refer to our guide *See How They Grow* at www.homeschoolmarketplace.com.

Write out lists of what each of the following subjects will cover during Suzie's sixth grade year:

Bible Study

Family Involvement

Community Involvement

Household Management

Typing

Basic Computer Knowledge

Basic Entrepreneurship

Fine Arts

Music

Step 4. Compile a master list from the typical course of study and the lists you made for the new subjects you've added to Suzie's course of study.

Step 5. Roughly decide the time frame in which you are going to cover all the topics on your list during the school year.

Step 6. Following the same process, create a course of study for each of your children.

Good work! You now have a year's course of study (scope and sequence) for each of your children.

This chapter was written by Ellyn Davis and is excerpted from her e-book **Creating Your Own Course of Study** *available at www.homeschoolmarketplace.com.*

10

THE HIGH SCHOOL YEARS

THE HIGH SCHOOL YEARS are when many parents stop teaching their children at home. These parents feel overwhelmed by the demands of high school subjects, feel unqualified to teach upper level math and sciences, and begin wondering if their children need the social exposure and athletic opportunities available in public and private high schools. Also, there is the question of accreditation and transcripts for students wishing to go to college.

Last, but not least, during the high school years children tend to express themselves much more independently and it would be easier for parents to let someone else require schoolwork from a teen who is going through mood swings or becoming argumentative.

If I do nothing else, I want to encourage you to keep your child at home during the high school years if at all possible.

If you find your resolve drooping, your vision dimming, your enthusiasm waning, watch Josh Harris's video *Why Home School Through High School* or listen to my seminar on *Charting a Course for High School*, or read *Dumbing Us Down* by John Gatto. The teen years are crucial to the identification and legitimizing of a child, and we can't afford to let others set our children's life course for them.

Plus, the teen years are when home schooling parents begin seeing the fruit of their labors of home schooling the early years. As your children move toward adulthood, their relationship with you can begin changing from "child" to "friend," and that is a precious experience you don't want to miss.

OPTIONS FOR HIGH SCHOOL

There seem to be three common teaching options for high school. First, the textbook route. Parents who want their children to go to college and who are unsure about how to cover all the requirements at home often choose to buy each year's curriculum from a Christian publisher who produces textbooks or videos with textbooks that parallel the scope and sequence of the public schools. The second option is the non-textbook route, where the necessary core subjects and electives are covered by using alternative, non-textbook resources. The final option is a combination of textbooks and alternative resources which together cover all essential requirements.

There are four basic decisions that must be made no matter which teaching option is chosen:

Envision the child's future. Most parents can tell by the time their child is 12 or 13 whether he/she is suited for a profession or trade. This is when we have to be realistic. Even though we might want our son to become a doctor or lawyer, he might do better as an auto mechanic. We need to map out the high school years as a "career pathway" that lays a foundation for what will serve our sons and daughters well as adults. If college is in their future, there are certain course requirements that must be met. If college is not in their future, there are still state requirements that must be met and an emphasis on certain courses important to the child's future. Your state Board of Education can provide you with high school course requirements, and your state's Board of Regents has a list of college entrance requirements for statewide colleges and universities.

Map out a course of study. The average high school credit requires 100 hours of study. This study can be accomplished through textbooks or through independent projects you devise yourself. If using a non-traditional approach, you will have to decide your own course requirements such as: What will this course entail? What will have to be done for the work to be considered completed? What con-

---

IF I DO NOTHING ELSE, I WANT TO ENCOURAGE YOU TO KEEP YOUR CHILD AT HOME DURING THE HIGH SCHOOL YEARS IF AT ALL POSSIBLE.

---

stitutes an A, a B, a C in this course? Some parents gear the course work to the PSAT, SAT, ACT, or achievement tests and "teach to the tests," others cover the required number of course credits in a way that best suits their family.

Devise a record keeping system. You will need to devise some sort of transcript that shows the number of credits in each subject and the grades in each course. The closer you can make this look like a traditional high school transcript, the better. It also helps to keep a portfolio of selected projects and a list of extracurricular activities like church work, 4-H, apprenticeship opportunities, Scouting, community involvement, etc. *The Home Schooler's High School Journal* is a good record keeping system for high school because it helps you keep track of credit hours in each course. Both *Relaxed Record Keeping* and *Creating Transcripts* have ideas for developing transcripts from non-traditional course work. You can also find sample highschool transcripts online.

Find out what your state homeschooling organization offers.
Our state organization arranges diplomas, graduation ceremonies, and
awards for graduating seniors. These not only give special recognition
to the graduates, but also give the kind of legitimacy to home schooling that is so reassuring to relatives and to the state. Your organization
may provide similar services.

How Do We Earn Credits?

The number of high school credits needed for graduation vary from
state to state, but most states require a minimal number of credits in
core subjects in order for a student to graduate. This minimum requirements for most states are shown in the list below.

Credits Typically Required for High School Graduation

Language Arts 3 - 4

Science 2

Math 2 - 3

Social Studies 2 - 3

U.S. History 1

World History 1

Fine Arts 1

Foreign Language 1

Economics 1/2

Government 1/2

Physical Education (includes health) 2

Electives 7 - 9

What do these credits mean? Usually one credit in a particular
subject (for example, one credit in Language Arts) means that a class
was offered in that subject for 50 minutes each school day for a school

year (180 days) and that the student attended that class for 165 of the 180 days it was offered and performed work in that class to the teacher's satisfaction.

Let's examine the concept of a high school credit in more detail. Let's say your child needed one high school credit in Language Arts. If we multiply 50 minutes (the length of class time each day) by 150 days (the number of days the student actually attended the class, assuming the student was allowed 15 absences a year and another 15 classroom periods were spent with assemblies, pep rallies, substitute teachers, non-learning activities, etc.) we get 126 hours of actual class (and field trip) time toward that credit. However, we know that in a typical classroom less than half of the time is spent in learning activities. The other half is spent settling down the class, discussing assignments, taking up or giving out papers, dealing with trouble-makers, and so on.

This means that out of that year of class time in Language Arts, teaching (and presumably learning) was actually occurring for less than 63 hours. Add 20 minutes of homework in that class three days a week and that adds another 36 hours of learning time. So a high school credit actually reflects roughly 100 hours of work in a particular subject, if that much. (When we have talked to former high school teachers, they agree that 100 hours is a generous estimate.)

The second thing we need to examine is what a credit of work in a subject represents. For example, if our subject is Language Arts, usually the high school level courses are such things as "Survey of Western Literature," or "American Literature," or "Short Stories, Poetry, and Plays," or "Theater," or "Public Speaking," or a general course that includes grammar and composition. The goal for each literature course is for the student to become familiar with the major works of a particular literary genre and to have some understanding of the plot structure of novels, the metric structure of poetry, and the presentation of a play. The goal for the grammar and composition courses is the ability to communicate clearly and persuasively through writing using correct spelling, grammar, punctuation and capitalization, and the goal for the public speaking course would be to communicate clearly and persuasively when speaking to a group.

Now that we have some understanding of both the amount of time that is involved in earning one high school credit and the goal of the subject studied for that credit, we can develop our own course outlines.

Non-traditional methods of earning high school credits

Suppose we wanted to develop a course similar to a "Survey of Western Literature." We would begin with books that list the literature major colleges consider most important for high school students to read like *Reading Lists for the College Bound* or *Invitation to the Classics*. We would also find books on using discernment in reading, such as *Reading Strands* or *How to Read a Book*. If we picked ten books that represented the best in Western literature over a broad time span, had our child read those books, write brief essays about each according to the ideas in *How to Read a Book* or discuss each following the format given in *Reading Strands*, this could easily take 100 hours and earn one high school credit in Language Arts. We would represent that credit hour on our home-made transcript as "Survey of Western Literature."

As far as grades are concerned, we are free to establish our own guidelines, since that's what school teachers do. In a public school, the teachers are free to decide how they will grade their classes (how much credit for homework, for tests, for classroom participation, for the final exam, etc.) and they are also free to choose whether they will grade "on the curve" (which means grades are determined by the class average) or on a strict numerical value.

One way we can grade would be on the effort expended and the quality of the papers and discussion. If this seems too subjective, we could clearly define grading before the course began in ways like: read 10 books and write/give 10 reports equals an A; 8 books and 8 reports equals a B; 6 books and 6 reports equals a C, and so on.

Because our student is earning a course credit based on spending 100 hours of time, this 100 hours can be spread over two weeks, two months, or two years. When and how the credit is earned is not the issue; covering the material is. We could even design the course so that

---

HIGH SCHOOL CREDITS CAN BE EARNED IN OTHER WAYS THAN THROUGH READING BOOKS OR STUDYING CURRICULUM MATERIALS. INVOLVEMENT IN ACTIVITIES OUTSIDE THE HOME CAN ALSO BE COUNTED AS CREDITS TOWARDS GRADUATION.

---

it provides only half a credit. In high schools with a semester system, courses are often only given for one semester, so they count for half a credit each. Half a credit courses are even easier for home schoolers to design because they only represent 50 hours or less of work.

A lot of high schools and colleges have developed summer school courses that are only two to three weeks long. Students concentrate intensively on one or two subjects for those few weeks and get a full semester's credit. This format could easily be followed in the home school.

High school credits can be earned in other ways than through reading books or studying curriculum materials. For example, one well-researched term paper can easily require 50 to 100 hours of work and be credited in Language Arts as "Grammar and Composition."

Involvement in activities outside the home can also be counted as credits towards graduation. Our children have all the Language Arts and Fine Arts credits in theater they will ever need because they have been in several productions at our community playhouse and each production requires at least 100 hours of rehearsal and performance time. They have an intimate understanding of the many aspects of presenting a play, from auditions, to memorizing a script, to making scenery, to setting props, and more.

Our boys also took dance classes and horseback riding lessons, and we counted the lessons and all practice as Physical Education. In addition, they also listen to many books on tape as we travel, and the listening and subsequent discussions in the car can be counted toward course work. Here are some examples of other non-traditional ways to earn high school credits:

• *"Career Choices."* Course requirements: Work through some of the books on career choices such as *Finding the Career That Fits You* or *48 Days to the Work You Love* and arrange to work for a set period of time as an apprentice in some of the careers that spark an interest.

• *"Shop."* Course requirements: Build something functional like bookcases, a table, a gardening shed, a stall in the barn, etc. Maintain some machinery, such as the lawnmower, the car, etc. Credit hours are given depending on the number of hours spent on the project.

• *"Economics."* Course requirements: Open checking and savings accounts. Manage these accounts faithfully for a specified period. Be responsible for purchasing for the household within certain categories (examples: food, clothing, gas) according to a budget. In addition there are many books on economics (a good, easy-to-read version is *Biblical Economics in Comics*).

• *"Philosophy."* Course requirements: Study the various world views influencing us today through such books as *Understanding the Times* or *The Universe Next Door*. Write a paper discussing your own worldview.

If you combined the world view study with a study of cultures and civilizations holding those worldviews and the historical rise of each world view, you could count this course as "World History."

• *"Public Speaking."* Course requirements: Join the 4-H public speaking club and attend their meetings. Enter the 4-H public speaking contest at the county level and be prepared to go on to the district and state levels. Alternate requirements: Prepare several speeches or talks and invite friends and family to come to hear you speak or prepare an audition piece for a play.

Many more ideas for developing course work and granting high school credits for all of your child's learning activities are found in the books *Senior High: A Home Designed Form-U-la* and *Homeschooling the High Schooler.* After all, if major universities grant credit for courses on *Star Wars* movies, why can't we grant high school credit for interests our children pursue?

WHAT ABOUT THE REALLY HARD COURSES?

Calculus, physics, chemistry, German—these are the types of courses parents usually feel inadequate to teach. However, foreign languages and higher level math and sciences are only an issue if the student plans to attend a four year college, and even then colleges vary in the number of credits they require. Most parents can tell by the time their child is 12 or 13 whether that child is college material, junior college material, technical school material, or "get-a-job" material.

Check with potential colleges to determine the actual number of credits required for acceptance. If the college requires a heavy load of credits in foreign languages and higher level math and sciences, all of these courses are available from traditional textbook publishers.

In addition, Abeka, The School of Tomorrow, and The Chalk Dust Company produce teaching videos in subjects like chemistry, physics, advanced algebra, calculus, and foreign languages. However, the easiest way to pick up course credits in these subjects is take them at your local community college.

Many home schoolers take their junior and senior years in high school at a community college under a dual enrollment plan and get both high school and college credit for their coursework.

STUDYING TO THE TESTS

Most prep schools design their senior high courses around preparing for the SAT or ACT. These schools are in the business of getting their students into Ivy League colleges, and the only way they can do this is to make sure the students score high on the tests that determine college admissions. Therefore the better high schools tend to "teach to the tests."

Home schoolers can take the same approach. We can get SAT and ACT test preparation books and design our senior high courses around preparing for these tests.

Another thing we can do is gear senior high courses to the CLEP or Advanced Placement Tests. These are tests the child takes that count for college credit. Many home schooling high school students (including the well-known Colfaxes whose sons received scholarships to Ivy League colleges) turn their high school years into studying for and taking one CLEP or Advanced Placement Test after another. By doing this, some of these students can exempt most of the course work in their first two years of college.

An excellent book of strategy for high schoolers is *How to Get Into the Top Colleges*. Written by people who run a consulting firm for parents who want their children admitted to the nation's best colleges, this book gives the inside story on what colleges look for and a step-by-step program for high school that virtually guarantees admission to any college.

BEYOND ACADEMICS

Christian home schoolers are interested in much more than academics, so our course of study for high schoolers might include the following in addition to the core curriculum:

Courses helpful for succeeding in the World:

•*Life Skills* (includes how to shop, drive a car, use a library, file an income tax form, read a financial report, read a map, fix a flat, basic machine maintenance, handling stress, conflict resolution skills, etc.)

•*Home Economics* (how to shop, do laundry, clean, cook, sew, and other skills associated with running a household)

•*Social Skills* (carrying on a conversation, manners, proper ways of addressing and interacting with people, some sort of social service)

•*Consumer Math* (basic everyday math including how to manage money, balance a checkbook, simple accounting, how to operate on a budget)

•*Self Understanding* (understanding of strengths and weaknesses, skills and deficiencies, proper ways of deriving self-esteem, etc.)

•*Logic and Thinking Skills* (recognizing fallacies in arguments and discussions, thinking clearly, etc.)

Courses helpful for succeeding in Family Life:

•*Marriage Preparation* (relating to a husband or a wife, childcare, sex education, handling marital stress, etc.)

•*Family Relationships* (the proper roles of husband, wife, and child, how to build rich family relationships)

Courses helpful for succeeding as an Employee:

•*Typing*
•*Office Management*
•*Computer Skills*

Courses helpful for succeeding as an Employer:
•*Social Skills* (includes same as above Social Skills plus how to motivate people, dealing with different kinds of workers, time management, marketing, developing long range plans, etc.)
•*Office Management Skills* (includes consumer math, typing, computer, and accounting skills, tax preparation, ability to read a financial report)

Courses helpful for succeeding as a Christian:
•*Bible and Spiritual Studies* (how to study the Bible and use a concordance or Bible study helps, reading of biographies of Christians, applying biblical principles to everyday life, developing of character)
•*Understanding of Gifting* (recognizing God-given spiritual abilities and talents, knowing "who I am" spiritually)

BUT WHAT ABOUT COLLEGE?

Many home schooling parents are not sure their children should go to college. One of the reasons is the cost, which can easily run more than $25,000 a year for room, board, and tuition.

Another reason is that most colleges nurture world views and behaviors that are in conflict with all that Christian home schooling parents try to instill in their children. It doesn't make sense to spend eighteen years instructing a child and then send that child to a place that undermines all you have taught.

A third reason is that graduating from college no longer means that a person is highly educated. More than half of all college seniors fail general knowledge tests of basic history and literature.

Also, a college education no longer guarantees financial success, nor is a degree essential to getting a good job. Seventy percent of all the jobs in the United States require only on-the-job training or some other form of alternative education. None of the twenty career fields listed by the U.S. Department of Labor as the fastest growing occupations require a four year degree. For these and other reasons many home schooling families are considering alternatives to college.

Harvey Unger in *But What If I Don't Want to Go to College?* says there are really only two good reasons to send a child to a traditional four-year college: First, the child has a deep desire to study academic subjects such as history, literature, or philosophy. Second, he has a deep commitment to career goals that require a four-year degree (such as medicine or law).

Parents should think twice before sending a child to college if the child is unclear about his future plans because statistics show 50% of college students take six years or more to get their four year degree. Some of these students take longer to graduate because they are working their way through, but many of them take an extra two years to finish because they have no clear idea of their future plans and so they keep changing majors along the way.

This means the parents are paying an extra ten to thirty thousand dollars or more because the child has no clear idea why he is going to college. Also, statistics show that fewer than 25% of those who earn college degrees actually find themselves working in their degree field. This is another reason to think twice before sending a child to college.

WHAT ARE THE ALTERNATIVES TO COLLEGE?

The most obvious choice is to simply get a job. A job may take the form of an internship, temporary work, working at home, self employment, or free-lancing. *What Color is Your Parachute* can help your student create a picture of his ideal job. Another resource is *Finding the Career That Fits You* from Larry Burkett's Christian Financial Concepts. This program will help your student identify his or her career gifts, talents, and interests.

A second option is to get specialized training. Alternative education is available through community colleges, vocational-technical schools, on-the-job training, etc. The book *But What If I Don't Want to Go to College?* lists the eleven types of alternative education available, gives the advantages and disadvantages of each, and includes guidelines for evaluating any program that you might find locally.

A third option is to home school through college. This is not as difficult as it may seem. *Bear's Guide to Non-Traditional Degrees* lists many universities requiring little or no residency. You can also design your own course of study and get college credit for your coursework because many colleges now give credits for life experiences and allow course exemptions based on high scores on advanced placement tests.

The fourth option is to help your young person start his own business. Several home schooling leaders suggest that launching your child into business is a better investment than paying for four years of college tuition. If the typical college education can cost upwards of a hundred thousand dollars, would a wiser use of that money be to invest in a business for your child, or better still, simply to invest the money?

One of the astonishing things about investments is that investment income can significantly dwarf employment income. What this means is that a consistent system of cautious investing over the long term (30 to 40 years) can result in much more money than the average person is able to earn in a lifetime.

A similar option to launching your child into business would be to use the college money to buy income-generating property, such as rental housing, duplexes, or apartments that your child can manage. This way he or she will not only have a place to live, but will also have an ongoing source of income, as well as his/her own property management business.

The final alternative is apprenticeship. Apprenticeship traditionally consisted of four stages. The novice observed an expert while generally assuming the role of a servant. He learned the technology and mastered the techniques of the craft.

A college education used to provide this stage of training but no longer does because it lacks any practical application of work.

The journeyman, so called because this stage originally involved travel, worked in several shops to master specialized applications of basic skills. The craftsman owned his own business, and, in direct pro-

> ONCE WE KNOW WHAT GOD CONSIDERS IMPORTANT, IT IS HELPFUL TO ALSO KNOW WHAT THE WORLD CONSIDERS IMPORTANT, SO THAT OUR CHILDREN CAN FUNCTION WELL "IN THE WORLD," WITHOUT BEING "OF THE WORLD."

portion to his ability to train others, became a master.

Choosing apprenticeship is a way to enter a profession without having to complete a standard four year degree.

PREPARING FOR ADULTHOOD

The end product of our home schooling efforts is for our children to be capable of assuming the adult responsibilities of a Christian man or woman. As we have studied the Bible, we've concluded that these responsibilities are:

The Biblical responsibilities of a man:

- To be a visible representative of God's nature

- To provide for his household

- To love and understand his wife

- To raise his children in the ways of God

- To provide leadership at home and in the community

- To participate in the Church of Jesus Christ

The Biblical responsibilities of a woman:

- To be a faithful example of a godly woman

- To respect, love, and be a helper to her husband

- To bear, nourish, and love children

- To creatively and effectively manage a household

- To teach younger women godly qualities

- To participate in the Church of Jesus Christ

Once we know what God considers important, it is helpful to also know what the world considers important, so that our children can function well "in the world," without being "of the world."

A recent survey of "What Employers Want" indicated that employers are looking for workers who can:

1. Manage their time. (arrive on time for work or appointments, use their on-the-job time productively, use their time to the advantage of the company)

2. Follow instructions. (do a job the way they have been shown or told, ask questions if they don't understand, change procedures only after asking permission, read and follow printed instructions, etc.)

3. Cooperate with others. (respect supervisors, get along with fellow workers, react constructively to conflict situations with customers, other employees, or bosses)

4. Demonstrate excellence and thoroughness in their work. (bring a job to quality completion, take pride in doing a good job, demonstrate motivation to achieve)

5. Show initiative. (recognize potential problems, see what needs to be done and do it without being told)

Because I have owned several businesses, I thoroughly agree with this list. Also, if you plan to own your own business you will need those employee skills, because you will essentially be your own employee until your business grows to the point where you can afford to hire others to help.

In addition, here is our "top five" list of abilities for those who plan to become bosses:

1. The ability to manage time. Not only to meet deadlines and get to appointments on time, but also to plan ahead so that what needs to be done gets done when it needs to get done and the ability to prioritize the use of our time. So often a home business becomes "the hobby that ate up our lives." Its demands can usurp family time, personal time, friend time, and God time if we are poor managers of our time.

2. The ability to handle stress. This includes knowing our limits physically, emotionally, spiritually, and financially; knowing how to relax, keeping the "big picture" in view when the details are driving you crazy, developing satisfying hobbies, constructively dealing with anger and time pressure, etc.

3. The ability to handle money. Owning your own business is always financially risky. Great care must be taken with money. Accumulating money can never be the primary motive for your business, because then you will make rash decisions out of fear or greed.

4. The ability to perform almost any office function. No matter what your business, if it grows you will eventually be doing word processing, data entry, spreadsheets, basic accounting, filing, data management, etc. It's easier to know how to do these things beforehand than it is to learn after you are already overwhelmed with responsibilities.

5. *The ability to get along with difficult people.* There will always be someone who rubs you the wrong way, who tries to take advantage of you, or who misinterprets your actions. Good social skills and knowing how to deal constructively with conflict are essential. If you have employees, you will also have to develop good people-management skills.

This chapter was written by Ellyn Davis and is excerpted from **Charting a Course Through High School**, *an e-book with much more comprehensive information about homeschooling a high schooler available at www.homeschoolmarketplace.com.*

11

AH...RELAX. Sounds good, doesn't it. Well, there's a way to "relax" in your home schooling efforts that brings the same "Ah" sigh of relief. I'm going to share with you how. To me, the heart of relaxed home schooling is a belief that God's intended plan for us all was to learn, live, and grow together as families. Although relaxed home schooling is somewhat unstructured, it is significantly different from "unschooling." The key points of relaxed home schooling are as follows:

• You are a family, not a school.
• You are a mom, not a teacher.
• You have individual relationships with your children; not a "relationship" to a class of students.
• You are free to set your own goals, rather than relying on someone else's ideas of "what you should be doing in third grade."
• You are free to select materials, choose methods, and create experiences whenever you want...at the start of the school year, or in April, or at 3:00 in the morning.
• You are free to think through where you are on the path to your goals in any way that makes sense to you...rather than being stuck in

91

a test, grade, label kind of mindset.

• You are free to get rid of the question, "What curriculum am I using?" and replace it with "What is going to work with THIS kid, THIS week, for THIS purpose?"

• You are free to lose all those lesson plans and teacher's guides, and you don't even necessarily have to know what you are doing tomorrow when you get up.

BUT...

• You do need to have an interesting lifestyle, filled with opportunities for learning and growing.

• You do need to know what your goals are, as a family and for each individual child.

• You do need to constantly assess the strengths, weaknesses, learning styles, personalities and goals of each child.

• You do need to recognize the changing needs of children, and adjust expectations and lifestyles as they get older.

• You do need to communicate with your husband what your goals are and where you are on the path to achieving them.

• You do need to maintain balance and have some kind of a stable schedule for your household.

• You do need to go to the public library regularly and read to the children a lot.

• You do need to find some like-minded individuals, or if there are none in your area, read about relaxed home schooling and communicate with others through e-mail or by phone so you don't feel so alone!

So, how do you do "relaxed home schooling?" That's what this chapter is about.

Relaxed Homeschooling with Young Children

Our society has drawn many lines and created boxes that I've never believed in. One such line is the magical transition that is supposed to take place around the age of six when a mother becomes too incompetent to continue working with her children and must send them off to school. The other is around the age of eighteen when a "child" mysteriously leaves the public school and becomes an adult overnight. I truly believe we can completely ignore those two supposed transi-

---

To me, the heart of relaxed home schooling is a belief that God's intended plan for us all was to learn, live, and grow together as families.

---

tions. However, there is one transition we can't ignore. That is the "line" children move across at about the age of twelve, when they leave childhood behind and become young transitional adults. (I don't believe in the concept of "teenager.")

For that reason, I tend to divide my talks into two categories: talking to those who have younger kids (defined as birth through twelve) and those who have older kids, twelve through adulthood.

For those of you with younger children, I really believe that ALL you need to do is be the absolutely best mother you can be, and provide them with a stable family life in a nurturing atmosphere with lots of real-life experiences and plenty of vicarious experiences in the form of good books, educational videos, etc.

I also believe, in this age of garbage, that one of your main roles is to shelter your younger kids from the damaging effects of such things as commercial television; junky movies; neighborhood children (from families that don't share your values); and everything else that brings "the world" to them before they are ready to handle it.

Whenever you have one of "those days", when your neighbor has just filled you in on the latest public school program, fully funded with your tax dollars, and you just KNOW you are damaging your children by denying them such wonderful learning experiences, remember that you are doing your kids a tremendous service by simply having them at home with you, even if you do happen to be a little "snippy" and crazy on occasion.

Remember the importance of setting those goals, too. My list consists of: values, habits, attitudes, skills, talents/interests, and knowledge. The first three are most important with young children. Build their character first, and the rest will follow. You don't need to do cute little unit studies to accomplish this, or place the "character word of the week" on a billboard in front of your school. You just need to live with them, week in and week out, and work on your own character. As you have successes, and make mistakes and apologize for them, the kids will learn along with you. Read the Bible every day for your own growth, and share the stories with the children. That's the way Jesus taught, through stories and parables.

Next, work on their attitudes. Because I know that it is far more important to me that I develop children who LOVE to read than teaching them disconnected reading skills, I can sense easily when it is time to stop anything I'm doing that is killing off their love of reading. Because I'm more interested in helping them to understand the value of communication than the value of diagramming sentences, I can focus on reading when they are younger, and recognize that all that writing can happen when they are older and more ready and willing to learn.

This doesn't mean you shouldn't help them learn to read, write, and do math! It just means your common sense and mother's intuition should always guide you more than some parenting book or curriculum guide.

When they say they want to learn to read, try some cheap phonics material and see if it works. If it does, fine. If it doesn't, back off, consider learning styles, and try something else (listen to my audio, *Reading and Writing the Natural Way* if this is a problem area). My daughter, Ginny, would never have learned to read through phonics. She just couldn't hear the sounds. I let her memorize the English language, instead, and she wound up graduating with an English degree from a private college.

What about math? In the early years, up through about fourth grade, I see no real need for curriculum at all. Instead, focus on real life math skills. Cook together, measure things, make a garden, go to the grocery store, buy them real watches, give them allowances and help them learn how to save, tithe, and spend, and all the math they really need at this age will come naturally. If you all enjoy them, a few math games can be a great addition to the curriculum.

There are lots of them around, and many aren't even labeled "math games", like *Monopoly*. If that one is too advanced for your child, consider *Knock Out* (the flip side of the *Muggins* game); addition or multiplication bingo games, or just hunt around at your local teacher store. If you happen to have a child who just LOVES workbooks, go to a local discount store and get something colorful, preferably with stickers. This approach will work BETTER than the planned curriculum materials available for this age. If you feel the need for a curriculum by fourth or fifth grade, take a look at something very basic, like Modern Curriculum Press or Horizons or Heath. Continue adding in lots of hands-on things and real life experiences, because they really need these all the way up through the elementary years.

In social studies and science, consider losing all the textbooks (which are dumb and boring and don't cover things in detail) and use a "relaxed unit studies" approach. You can either plan something in advance, or just go with the flow.. When your child finds a great spider web outside, go the library and get some books on spiders. Don't forget the fiction stories, either. Fiction stories about animals shaped my entire life. I still find myself saying hello to animals I pass on the street, talking to them as if they were people. (Yes, I'll admit it's weird, but I really relate better to animals than I do to people, and I credit it all to reading too many stories about animals when I was a kid.) Consider what kinds of hands-on experiences you can do for science. Make birdfeeders, create collections, go for nature walks, do nature journals or drawings, make a trail through a nearby woodsy area and create markers or a trail notebook to go with it. (My kids did this, and then tried to charge the neighbor kids to walk down the trail....secondary lesson in economics.)

Do the same thing with history/social studies. Follow the news together, and learn about faraway places. Get videos about different countries or time periods. Read lots of historical fiction and/or biographies of famous people. Find some fun field trips to go on, and go with just your own family or maybe one other. (Avoid the crowds.)

Try to get some old-fashioned standards back into your life. Consider getting rid of your cell phones, and taking fewer outside classes when the kids are little. All those athletic programs and dance classes and outside academics can really wait until they are older. A few are fine. We even have some at our resource center, because younger children do like to have some time outside of the house with their peers. But watch the balance carefully! If you have five children and each of them has just one activity a week, they may each be in balance but YOU will be out of sorts playing chauffeur.

Try to spend almost every morning at home. Add in some old-fashioned activities, even if you live in the middle of a city, like gardening during the early morning hours, or grinding your own grain and baking bread from scratch. Get out the old sewing machine and learn how to actually make something. These old skills really have a way of settling you down and reminding you of what life should really be like. Also, seriously consider getting rid of the television completely. If you don't, severely limit the amount and type of TV watched. Television

> **The years from about fifth grade through eighth grade are meant as a transition from the carefree, family-style existence I've been portraying to the somewhat more structured high school scene.**

is getting trashier all the time, and we finally cut off the cable a few months ago and are a lot happier (except we miss the Braves games). Do the same thing with the Nintendo junk.

Okay. I know I'm getting preachy. I'll stop. But I really believe that the modern-day media is threatening to destroy our kids and our family lives, and I, for one, am ready to go back to a simpler time. So whatever makes sense to you, try at least one thing from the above list, and see if you don't agree, at least a little bit. Or am I just turning into an old fogey?? Tell me if you think I'm wrong!

The Middle Years: Filling in the Gaps

The years from about fifth grade through eighth grade are meant as a transition from the carefree, family-style existence I've been portray-

97

ing to the somewhat more structured high school scene.

This is an age for filling in gaps. Take a look at your long-range goals and see what happened naturally when they were younger, and what looks like weaknesses or areas where they have no interest whatsoever. Then think through the relative importance of those areas, and decide what needs attention.

At our resource center, the middle school classes are all designed to fill in gaps and prepare for high school. One of our classes, for example, is a creative writing class, because as many of you know, writing comes easily to some and is very tough for others. Another class is called "preparation for algebra," and is meant to solidify basic concepts like fractions, decimals, percents, and consumer math before moving on to abstractions.

The middle years are also a time for moving gradually out from the shelter of the family cocoon and finding ways to interact with members of a larger community. Volunteer experiences, mentorships, and apprenticeships might be things to consider, especially after the age of 12 or 13. Some kids that age begin their own businesses. At 12, my son Steve had his own "pet-sitting business," where he took care of people's pets when they went on vacation. This may also be a good time to consider doing some of the things you didn't have time for earlier, like sports programs or outside classes. Above all, recognize that these kids are becoming young adults as they pass that "12-year old" line, and have needs that are changing. You must adjust your "philosophy" as necessary. If you still have younger children, you need to keep them in balance, too, but those older kids are not going to be satisfied anymore being dragged around to little kid's activities, and assigned too many babysitting duties. They need to get out of the house on their own once in awhile, even if it is just being dropped off at the library to have some time alone. (I'm talking about a seventh grader, now, when I'm talking about leaving them alone....not a fifth grader...big difference in those two ages, both in terms of reality and society's perception.)

If you have trouble understanding your middle schooler, consider listening to my audio, "Beat the Middle School Blahs." There are lots of changes at this age, and the better you understand them, the better you will all survive the experience!

And then we come to High School!

Just because you come to the high school years does not NECESSARILY mean you need to get all structured and subject-oriented. However, you need to understand your options at this level, because the choices you make will affect the ease with which your kids can enter college later.

However, it is still important to treat them as individuals. My oldest son, Sam, never did any structured classes, did not have a "traditional transcript," never even "took" any science in high school, and eventually graduated with a degree in geology/minor in biology from a public university. However, with his unconventional education, he had to go a circuitous route to get into college. He went to a private school first, and then transferred into the public university. Dan, on the other hand, had an impeccable transcript. He liked structure, enjoyed textbooks, and took all the classes he could at our resource center.

Ginny, my oldest daughter, graduated early and went to college at sixteen, and Laura, who is now sixteen, isn't even sure college is in her future. In other words, they are all different, and they simply can't be treated as clones just because we are scared that we will somehow mess them up for life if their transcripts aren't adequate.

However, if your students are willing and it's going to work for you, it may be more important to "declare" subjects in high school.

However, just because you are "taking biology" doesn't mean you have to do it exactly like a public school would in order to justify the credit. Anything that is "lab" just means it has significant hands-on work involved, outside of textbook learning. Recently, I overheard a teenager and her mother arguing about whether or not her chemistry had been "lab." The mother was saying, "But, honey, every time we bake in the kitchen, that's lab.".....Well, no. I sided with the daughter. Simply baking is great when they are little, but that's not good enough for high school. But if you consciously learned about the chemistry involved in baking, it could be!

Similarly, if you are trying to get in your foreign language require-ment, you could get a typical two-year course, from someplace like Bob Jones or Power Glide, and do it that way, OR you could learn Spanish through missionary work, or go to Germany for a year as an au pair, like one of my friend's kids did.

Declaring subjects does not, in itself, mean you can no longer be creative or relaxed! However, by the high school years, you do need to focus on the areas of skills and knowledge from the list of goals. Some of the skills I think are important to cover would include:

• Communication skills, especially speaking in public and writing on a college level: persuasive essays; comparison-contrast papers; term papers; etc.
• Computer skills, especially word processing and internet re-search
• Old-fashioned library research skills
• Computational ability. If you are college-bound, that means at least through Algebra I and Geometry and preparation for the math por-tions of the SAT or ACT.
• Organizational skills, such as outlining, note-taking, scheduling

• Money management skills

• Other life skills, and a "can-do attitude" towards new experiences

If you want to declare subjects, and are going to a college that really cares about the list being comprehensive, here is a typical one. One credit is typically given for a class that is attended once a day for a year in a traditional school, to give you a "feel" for what it means.

JUST BECAUSE YOU COME TO THE HIGH SCHOOL YEARS DOES NOT NECESSARILY MEAN YOU NEED TO GET ALL STRUCTURED AND SUBJECT-ORIENTED.

• Four credits of English. Be sure they include some components of grammar, composition, U.S. Literature, and British or World Literature.

• Four credits of math, including Algebra I, Geometry, Algebra II, and something beyond Algebra II. I recommend Pre-Calculus.

• Four credits of Science, including Physical Science; Biology (lab); Chemistry (lab); and either Physics or Advanced Biology (Anatomy and Physiology). I personally recommend Jay Wile's *Apologia* series, except the physics may be too math-oriented for some people.

• Four credits of social studies, including U. S History; World History; Government and Economics (semester of each); and an elective. (We do "World Geography and Missions.")

• Two credits of foreign language. (Usually should be the same foreign language, preferably taken near the end of high school, and usually they don't count sign language.)

• Enough electives, often taken 2 credits at a time, from such areas as art, music, comparative religion, Bible, etc. so that the total number of high school credits adds up to at least 22 credits.

Be sure to remember to prepare for and take the SAT or ACT, preferably a couple of times, starting whenever a student feels adequate in algebra and geometry.

Finally, I'd like to remind you all of the biggest danger to the home schooling movement today...the push towards accreditation. Stay away from it!!!! Fight it!!!! Right now, it is not necessary to be accredited. I've NEVER had any trouble helping any student enter college without such accreditation and I've worked with literally hundreds! However, if enough people buy into "accreditation," it may become necessary and then ALL our control will be gone and we no longer will be able to relax and be families!

This chapter was written by Mary Hood and reprinted with permission from the Summer, 2003 issue of "The Relaxed Home Schooler's Newsletter." Mary Hood and her husband, Roy, home-schooled their five children and have seen their children successfully make the transition from homeschool to college and adult life. Mary has a Ph.D. in education, and is a nationally-known speaker and the author of such books as **The Relaxed Home School**, **The Joyful Home Schooler,** *and* **The Enthusiastic Home Schooler.**

12

I LOVE FIREWORKS, and each year around the fourth of July in our little town in Tennessee you can find a fireworks tent on every major street corner. Thank God that fireworks are still legal in Tennessee!

Ever since the boys were very small, I would take them to one of the fireworks tents the week before the Fourth and let them pick out an assortment of fireworks. Blake always chose smoke bombs or those intricate, machine-like fireworks, like the tanks that you light and they move around puffing smoke before exploding. James liked sparklers and Roman Candles and bottle rockets, and Seth usually went for the biggest "boom" he could find. And, of course, they all liked firecrackers.

On the actual day of the Fourth, we usually had a cookout with friends and went to watch the city fireworks display. Then came the best part. We would come home, have dessert, and then create our own fireworks extravaganza. And we always made sure that we read the *Declaration of Independence* sometime during the festivities.

Every time we would read the *Declaration of Independence*, we would be sobered to think that a group of men were so dedicated to their vision of freedom that they were willing to pledge their "lives, their fortunes, and their sacred honor" to see that vision become a reality. And many of those who signed the *Declaration* did lose their lives, their fortunes, and their sacred honor.

THE BIG SECRET ABOUT HOME SCHOOLING

With that in mind, I want to let you in on THE big secret about home schooling. Home schooling is either the easiest thing you've ever done, or the hardest, depending on how stressful it is for you to trust God, trust yourself, and trust your kids and how comfortable you are with freedom of choice. Once, at a home school convention, a lady spoke to Chris and she hit the nail right on the head. She said, "You know why home schooling is so hard? It's because of the FREEDOM we have."

Underlying all the other reasons we might have chosen to home school is the desire to have the FREEDOM to direct and nurture the course of our children's lives—including their education.

Freedom is scary. It makes us want boundaries, rules and regulations so we always know exactly what to do and exactly where our kids stand compared to everybody else's kids.

It's like being a Christian, isn't it? As a Christian we can choose rules or a relationship. Being legalistic is easy, because we know what we have to do to be "acceptable" to God and we can gauge whether we are doing better or worse than we are "supposed" to do. We can also gauge whether we're doing better or worse than other Christians we know. But living out of a true relationship with God can be very difficult if we like rules. Why? Because we're not in charge of the standards any more. Only God's opinion matters, and He tends to judge by the spirit of the law, not the letter.

Because it's always easier to rely on external measurements and comparisons with others to know if we are doing things "right," home schooling parents tend to gradually drift toward some imitation of the public or private (let us say "institutional") school, just like a Christian will always tend to drift toward some form of legalism. We like the safety of having a system as well as the security of knowing where we stand at all times. Plus, it's always easier to have someone else figure things out for us, whether that someone else is our pastor or a curriculum publisher.

So, what's the point of this chapter? A gripe session? No. I want to

> **HOME SCHOOLING IS EITHER THE EASIEST THING YOU'VE EVER DONE, OR THE HARDEST, DEPENDING ON HOW STRESSFUL IT IS FOR YOU TO TRUST GOD, TRUST YOURSELF, AND TRUST YOUR KIDS AND HOW COMFORTABLE YOU ARE WITH FREEDOM OF CHOICE.**

commend all of you who are teaching your children at home. I want everyone who reads this essay to know that I understand how scary and hard home schooling can be. First, it goes against every experience we have regarding what education is. Second, it opens us up to a lot of criticism from family and friends. Third, we feel insecure about our ability to pull it off and fourth, we are uncomfortable about using our children as "guinea pigs" while we figure out what we are doing.

Just to attempt home schooling requires a huge leap of faith. In fact, if we are unable to home school "in faith" we might as well send our children to the government (or Church) school.

But I also want you to know that it IS possible to home school in "freedom." We haven't done everything perfectly (by earthly standards), but we've home schooled for over 20 years with our three boys and God has blessed us beyond our wildest hopes. They may not know all the names and dates our minds were crammed full of in public school, but they are responsible, productive, on-fire for God, interesting people who love their families and friends.

This doesn't mean you can't assign grade levels (we didn't). This doesn't mean you can't have a plan (we did). What it means is that you recognize the whole manmade industry of institutional "schooling" for what it is: a lie. John Gatto says (and we agree with him), "School was a lie from the beginning. It continues to be a lie."

Don't buy into the lie just because it's harder not to. For some reason, God has placed in your heart a desire to home school your children. YOU find out why. YOU find out how. Be FREE to do what you find out.

You don't need an impressive educational background or lots of money to succeed at homeschooling. Research has shown that parents with only a high school education are capable of doing as good a job at educating children as their professional teacher counterparts or those with advanced degrees. Research has also shown that those who spend less than $200 per child per year on home school curriculum materials can produce results as good or better than those who spend two to three times that amount.

So relax and enjoy your freedom. You CAN do it.

Part Two

Teaching the
Major Subjects

I CARVED THE ANGEL
FROM THE MARBLE

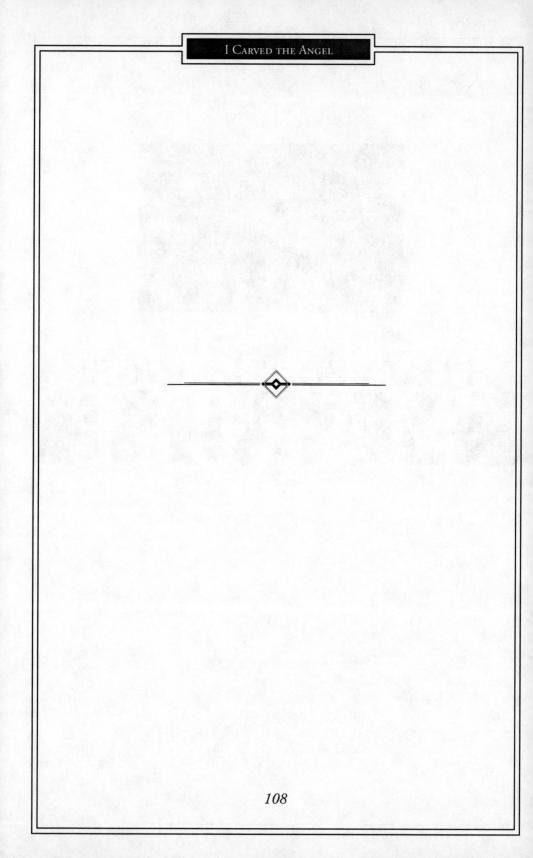

13

TEACHING LANGUAGE ARTS

LANGUAGE ARTS IS CONCERNED WITH COMMUNICATION: communicating with others through writing or speaking, and receiving communication from others through reading or listening. All of the various subjects studied in Language Arts, such as phonics, grammar, handwriting, spelling, vocabulary, etc. are nothing more than tools for effective reading, listening, writing, and speaking. The different subjects assume their proper emphasis when we see them for what they are—tools that help our children communicate well with others.

In grades one through six, language arts programs focus on these core areas, usually in this order:

1. Listening, Speaking, and Visual Discrimination Skills

2. Decoding Words and Phonics

3. Handwriting

4. Written Expression (composition)

5. Reading Comprehension

6. Spelling

7. Grammar and Usage (basic grammar, capitalization, punctuation)

8. Vocabulary Development

9. Study Skills and Information Resources

10. Appreciating Literature and Language

In junior high grades, emphasis is on these core areas:

1. Grammar and Usage

2. Spelling

3. Composition

4. Vocabulary Building

5. Reference and Study Strategies

6. Refining Listening, Speaking, and Viewing Skills

7. Literature and Reading

At the high school level, language arts is concerned with the same core areas as in junior high, but each area is covered in more depth.

READING

Perhaps the most traumatic event for home schooling parents is teaching a child to read. It is traumatic not because it's hard to do, but because we have been brainwashed into thinking our children will be ruined forever if we use the wrong reading program or if they don't learn to read when they are 6 years old. Reading is such an important issue, and choosing a reading program is such an emotionally charged topic, let's examine both the subject of reading and the types of phonics programs available.

What do we want to communicate to our children about reading?
There are four main concepts we want to communicate about reading:

(1) Written words have value because they are a vital communication tool;

(2) Written words can be personally enjoyable;

(3) Written words increase understanding and power over the world;

(4) Reading is something most people can easily learn to do.

We communicate these concepts through:

(1) *Having a print rich environment.* This simply means our house is full of good things to read. *Cradles of Eminence* studied common factors in the childhoods of 400 eminent men and women and concluded: "A rule of thumb for predicting success is to know the number of books in the home."

(2) *Reading aloud to the child from an early age,* pointing out simple words, running a finger from left to right under the lines of print, and encouraging the child that soon he will be able to read these books himself.

(3) *Letting the child see you read.* Children take their cues about what is worthwhile from their parents. If the parents seldom read, the children assume reading is not a valuable activity. Boys need to see their fathers read.

(4) *Letting the child see you attach value to books.* This not only means that you have your own library of personal "treasures," but it also means that the child sees you go to books for answers to questions you have. One reason boys tend to read less than girls is that boys seldom see their fathers attach importance to reading.

Do we need a reading program?

Yes and No. Many children seem to learn to read all by themselves, but others need guidance. Those who need to be taught to read will tend to fall into three categories: (1) easy readers who only need a minimum of instruction; (2) children who need a good, "no frills" phonics program, and (3) children who need a program with lots of reinforcement.

Choosing a reading program

A child's first experiences with reading will set a tone of like or dislike of books (and of learning) for years to come. For that reason parents need to be very careful about introducing reading. There are three factors to a good first reading experience: readiness, learning style, and the teacher's attitude.

A CHILD'S FIRST EXPERIENCES WITH READING WILL SET A TONE OF LIKE OR DISLIKE OF BOOKS (AND OF LEARNING) FOR YEARS TO COME.

---

(1) *Readiness* is a crucial factor in a child's ability to learn and in his attitude toward learning. Readiness means that the child is mentally and emotionally capable of assimilating the information presented; he/she has enough life experiences for the information to be meaningful; and he/she has minimal frustration in acquiring the skill or performing the required tasks.

The two subject areas in which a child's readiness is most often violated are language arts and math. Because we home schooling parents are subject to peer pressure and because most states require testing, we tend to push our children in reading, writing, and math. The result can be frustrated children and frustrated parents.

The best kind of learning has four ingredients: (1) maturity (the physical, mental, and emotional ability to process the information or perform the assigned task); (2) experience (enough general knowledge about the subject to provide a base on which further knowledge can be added); (3) a desire to learn (a receptivity to the information); and (4) a system (an effective way of presenting the information).

How do we apply the four ingredients of successful learning to teaching the skill of reading?

The maturity necessary for reading involves being able to hear language distinctly and distinguish between letter sounds. It also requires the visual acuity to focus on a printed page without eyestrain or visual confusion.

The experience necessary to reading involves understanding that letters stand for sounds and that groups of letters "say" something. Children routinely make these connections by themselves and begin asking "What does that say?"

Next comes the desire to learn. Most children begin wanting to know how to read sometime before age 8. Once they really want to read they can learn at an astonishing rate. Some even teach themselves.

The final component of meaningful learning is a system such as a good phonics program.

(2) *Learning Style.* Some children learn best by hearing, some by seeing, and some by doing. Reading is by nature a visual activity, but it helps some children to have songs, games, or "hands-on" activities.

(3) *The Teacher's Attitude* has a powerful effect on the student's success. A child learning to read should not have to deal with feelings of inadequacy, being compared to others, or a teacher whose ego is wrapped up in the student's ability to read.

Remember, your goal is not just to produce a reader, your goal is to produce a reader who enjoys reading and learning.

ELEMENTS OF PHONICS

There are basically 44 sounds (phonemes or phonograms) in the English language, and phonics programs teach children to read by familiarizing them with single letter sounds and the sounds of letters in combination.

Most phonics programs start with letter recognition. Once the child can recognize his A, B, Cs and knows the sound each letter makes (usually starting with the short vowel sounds), he will start making short words which follow a consonant-vowel-consonant pattern such as *rap*, *top*, *cut*, etc. The next step will be to introduce consonant blends (two or three consonants together): *rap* becomes *scrap*. Then the child usually learns the long vowel sounds by adding a silent *e* to the end of a word: *scrap* becomes *scrape*.

The rest of the phonics course is devoted to digraphs (two letters that together make one sound such as *th, ch, sh, wh, ui, ay, oe*); diphthongs (two vowels that make a distinctive sound such as *oi, ou*); combinations that make their own sound (such as *ould, igh, tion*); R-controlled words (such as *car, fern, nurse*); and sight words that are not phonetic like *the*.

READING PLATEAUS

Reading teachers have found there are three predictable plateaus a child will reach where learning seems to "stall out" for a time before the child can go further. The first plateau is learning the alphabet, the second is at the letter blending stage, and the third is at the long vowel stage when silent *e* is added. Many teachers find that once a child passes the long vowel stage, he seems to "take off" and sails through the rest of the program.

Reading instruction for home schoolers seems to follow the "3 Rule." If your child has difficulty learning to read, no matter which reading programs you try, the third one usually works. It works, not because it's the best of the three, but because by the time you try the third one you are more confident and your child has assimilated everything taught in the first two.

TYPES OF PHONICS PROGRAMS

Phonics programs come in many sizes, shapes, and prices, but are all variations of common themes:

Theme #1: "Ladder Letters." Ladder Letter programs teach letter combinations in the following format: *ba* ("baa"), *be* ("beh"), *bi* ("bih"), *bo* ("bah"), *bu* ("buh"), with a consonant or consonant blend before the vowel. To make a word, the child would then add an ending consonant to the *ba, be, bi, bo, bu* to make *bat, bet, bit, bot,* and *but. Sing, Spell, Read, and Write* is an example of a Ladder Letter phonics program.

Theme #2: "Word Families." Word Family programs are also called Linguistic Approaches. The linguistic approach has been found to be more effective than Ladder Letters because it teaches the child to read according to the way words are usually broken into syllables. The child is taught to read word families such as *an, at, am, en, it* and then beginning consonants or consonant blends are added to the word family. For example, the word family *at* is used to form *bat, cat, dat, fat, gat, hat, lat, mat, nat, pat, rat, sat, vat, wat* and the child sounds them out as *b-at, c-at, f-at,* etc., not as *ba-t, ca-t, fa-t* like in the Ladder Letter approach. Even the nonsense words like *lat* are syllables of larger words like *latitude. Alpha-Phonics* and Bob Jones Press use a word family approach.

Theme #3: "Bells and Whistles" or "Bare Bones." Some phonics programs have games, songs, prizes, and many other extras that enhance the basic phonics teaching, others just stick to straight phonics. The "Bells and Whistles" programs claim that their fun, colorful, multiple-reinforcement approach makes learning to read easier and more pleasant for children and teachers. The "Bare Bones" programs claim that no frills are necessary, and that all the extras prolong the teaching process, distract from reading, and needlessly increase the price of the program.

Theme #4: "Rule Based" versus "Reading Based." Some programs teach phonics according to spelling rules and claim that teaching this way makes children better spellers. *The Writing Road to Reading* and *Phonics for Reading and Spelling* are rule-based reading programs. "Reading Based" programs focus more on getting the child reading, bringing in rules when they apply, but not making them the focus of the reading pro-

---

SOME PARENTS MISTAKENLY BELIEVE

THAT ONCE A CHILD CAN READ HE

IS THEN READY TO BEGIN LEARNING

ON HIS OWN THROUGH READING.

---

gram. They claim that rule-based programs frustrate young children and squelch their natural desire to read. There is also evidence that rule-based programs produce poorer readers because the rules act as "censors" in the children's minds as they read, slowing them down and dulling comprehension.

LEARNING TO READ VERSUS READING TO LEARN

Some parents mistakenly believe that once a child can read he is then ready to begin learning on his own through reading. However, most children cannot read to learn until about the fourth grade.

There are three skills necessary in order to enjoy reading and to benefit from it. *The first is automaticity.* It takes at least 20 minutes of reading a day for several years before reading becomes automatic. Until automaticity is reached, a child will be too focused on decoding to glean much content from what he is reading.

The second skill is visualization. The ability to picture in one's mind what is being read enhances comprehension and memory. Parents can help a child learn to visualize by reading vivid passages aloud, stopping frequently to ask the child to describe what is being read. Another way to develop visualization is to read picture books to a child without letting him see the pictures, ask him what he imagines the pictures look like, then compare his imagination to the artist's illustrations.

Finally, *the child must have enough of an experience base* for what he is reading to make sense to him. Children with a wider range of experiences, such as travel, attending plays and musical performances, visiting museums, and interacting with a variety of people learn to read more quickly and have greater reading comprehension.

Usually it takes a child until fourth grade to have reached a level of automaticity, to have acquired the visualization skills, and to have accumulated a broad enough base of life experiences to begin learning through reading. Girls tend to be better early readers and more active readers. Boys usually do not become independent readers who read for pleasure until they are aged ten or older. Part of the reason for this is that boys usually have more frustrating learning-to-read experiences than do girls because early schooling concentrates on reading, writing, and linguistic activities that favor the fine motor skills and verbal abilities of girls.

LISTENING AND OBSERVING

Instructional settings, such as school, tend to focus on only two aspects of language arts: reading and writing. However, most communication between people is verbal or visual, through conversation and body language. These verbal and visual communication channels are extremely important because they can be easily misunderstood and account for most "failure to communicate." Marriage and family counselors report that their patients' top two complaints have to do with communication. Number one is that people don't think loved ones listen to them, and number two is that their loved ones misunderstand what is said. Listening and observing are skills that can be learned and practiced at home from the time children are very small.

SPEAKING

In our grandparents' day, children practiced elocution and debate from grammar school up. Young ladies were taught how to speak pleasantly with correct diction, and young men were trained in public speaking. Sadly, nowadays the only place you are likely to see such instruction is through the 4-H Public Speaking program. Students mumble, slur their words, use "like" or "you know" as an introduction to every phrase, and communicate extensively with slang terms ("That, like, you know, really bums me out.") Not only does this inability to speak correctly cause communication problems, but it causes employers untold headaches because it has become very difficult to find employees who use proper speech patterns and conversational skills when interacting with customers.

WRITING

The foundation of writing is penmanship, or handwriting, in which the student learns to write the alphabet and eventually can write words and sentences in a pleasing, legible handwriting style.

Most handwriting programs begin with a simple form of lettering called manuscript. Usually by fourth grade, a modification of manuscript writing is introduced called cursive. In cursive writing, letters are slightly slanted, ascenders and descenders become loops instead of straight lines, and the letters within a word are joined together so there is no lifting of the pen or pencil between letters as in manuscript writing. Cursive is intended to be faster and easier to write than manuscript. Traditional handwriting alphabets have distinctly different manuscript and cursive scripts, but some of the more modern handwriting instruction uses scripts that are similar, so students have a smoother transition from manuscript to cursive writing. For example, DeNealian handwriting uses a "precursive," in which the manuscript letters are similar to the letters that will be used for cursive. Italic handwriting uses the same basic letter shapes for both manuscript and cursive, with cursive being formed by adding "joiners" to the manuscript letters.

A child can learn to write legibly with a minimum of frustration once his fine motor skills are sufficiently developed and if he practices until writing becomes automatic. Many boys have poorly developed fine motor skills well into fifth grade and find it very difficult to shape letters properly. This is one reason men tend to have poorer handwriting than women. Because of their late-blooming fine motor skills, boys also may have difficulty becoming "automatic" in their writing. In order to move on to independent writing assignments, a child must have mastered writing to the point that he or she no longer has to think about how to form the letters.

Once students have mastered handwriting, they are ready for more extensive writing assignments.

WRITING COURSES

Writing courses usually focus on two types of writing: *narrative writing* and *expository writing*.

Narrative Writing (also known as "Creative Writing") simply means "to write a story." This type of writing may either be fiction or non-fiction and is commonly introduced as soon as the child can commit thoughts to paper. It is called "narrative writing" because the writer narrates (tells or relates) the particulars of an event. The classic narrative writing assignment is a paper on "How I spent my summer vacation," but narrative writing can cover any form of story telling—from one paragraph to a short story to a novel. Journaling is also a form of narrative writing.

We try to begin all children with this kind of writing because we want a child's first writing experiences to be personally interesting. After all, what could be more interesting than a story about me? I know myself better than I know anyone or anything else and I have

---

**READ, READ READ, WRITE, WRITE, WRITE
AND TALK, TALK, TALK.**

---

had some pretty interesting (or exciting or sad) experiences. Who wouldn't want to read about me!

The easiest form of narrative writing to begin with when teaching children writing is to have them keep a journal. When they are really young, you can ask your child to tell you how he spent his day and write his journal for him. But as he gets older, the child can keep a journal on his own.

Expository writing is writing that explains. Instead of telling a story, expository writing explains something to the reader ("expository" means "to explain"). Examples of expository writing are: "How to train your dog;" "How to install a software program;" "Why I believe homeschooling is better than public schooling;" etc.

There are two types of expository writing: the research paper and the non-research paper. The research paper is usually assigned at the middle school through high school level and begins with a topic to investigate, a problem to solve, or a question to answer. A short research paper is referred to as a "report," while a longer paper involving extensive research is commonly called a "term paper." The conclusions shared in this type of writing are based on factual material gathered by the writer through a variety of resources, and the author must list and credit his or her sources of information. The author is expected to follow specific guidelines in the presentation of the paper and in the page layout.

The second type of expository writing involves little or no research. Two forms of non-research expository writing are the expository composition and the essay.

An expository composition explains, describes, or provides information on a topic. It tells what something is, what it is like, and/or how it works. An example of an expository composition would be a paper on "How to Bake Chocolate Chip Cookies."

An essay may also explain, describe, or provide information on a topic, but it does so in the context of presenting the author's opinions and personal experience concerning the topic. The most common essay form begins with a problem to solve or a question to answer (for example: "Are home schoolers properly socialized?") and then presents the writer's opinions concerning the problem/question in addition to supporting facts.

A report (such as a book report, news article, interview, etc.) may either be a research paper, an essay, or an expository composition, or may contain elements of all three.

Writing in the elementary grades usually focuses on narrative writing (writing stories or "creative writing") but also includes some expository writing in the form of reports—book reports and short research papers.

Since the ability to write expository papers (essays, reports and term papers) is so heavily emphasized in college, the high school years should be a time to focus more on expository writing, especially the ability to write research papers.

OVERWHELMED WITH OPTIONS?

Since reading and writing are the cornerstones of education (in other words, it's hard to study any other subject if you can't read or write), these subjects tend to be over-stressed.

Our recommendation is that you spend the early elementary years helping your child become an "automatic" reader and handwriter. Some basic instruction in parts of speech and capitalization and punctuation is helpful, but there is no substitute for actually reading and writing. In fact, studies have shown there is little correlation between the amount of grammar instruction a child receives and how correct his writing is. There is also little correlation in the early years between a child's ability to spell a word on a spelling test and his ability to spell it correctly in a composition

For those reasons, we say READ, READ, READ; WRITE, WRITE, WRITE; TALK, TALK, TALK; and LISTEN, LISTEN, LISTEN. A child who hears English properly used at home and consistently reads well-written literature will automatically internalize correct grammar, word usage, capitalization, punctuation, and spelling and will also develop an extensive vocabulary.

At the upper elementary and middle school level, reading and handwriting should have become automatic and you can begin more extensive writing assignments. High schoolers need to be perfecting research skills and essay writing and should have an in-depth grammar course. They also should be reading material that correlates with their future plans. For example, college-bound high schoolers can be reading from the recommended reading lists of the colleges they hope to attend.

This chapter was written by Ellyn Davis and is excerpted from the e-book **Teaching Language Arts at the Home** *available at www.homeschoolmarketplace.com.*

14

HELPING YOUR CHILD BECOME A LOVER OF BOOKS

IT IS HARD FOR US TO IMAGINE that literacy is a fairly new concept. Historically, only a select few were able to read. The original thrust towards universal literacy was a Protestant concept, designed to make the common man knowledgeable enough about the Bible to no longer rely upon a priestly caste for religious instruction. It is only in the past few centuries that reading has been considered a desirable activity for everyone.

Reading has changed our view of life in many ways: some good, some bad. Reading allows us access to information from across the globe. A book can bring us the combined wisdom and experience of multitudes from the present and the past. It can allow us to experience life outside of our sphere of existence.

But literacy has come at a great price. In many ways reading has become a substitute for personal interaction or experience. We can know all about someone through a book without having ever met him or her. Because we can now find what we need to know in books, we no longer need discipleship, the passing down of knowledge from the old and wise, or deep development of memory. Books do not hold us accountable for what we learn from them in the way people do.

Knowledge can now be "head knowledge" or "book learning," with no real experience behind it. So, when we strive to help our children become lovers of books, we need to know the risks involved and try to compensate for them.

THE IMPORTANCE OF READING GREAT BOOKS

C. S. Lewis once said, "We read to know we are not alone." What this means to me is that, through books, more than through any other medium, I can have conversations with the minds of other people—I can learn how they think, what they believe, what they value. And more

---

FROM AN EDUCATIONAL POINT OF VIEW,

BEING WELL-READ PLACES YOU IN THE

SMALL PERCENTAGE OF PEOPLE WHO HAVE

A BROADER PERSPECTIVE OF LIFE—THE

MOVERS AND SHAKERS OF THE WORLD.

---

importantly, I can discover more about myself. There is something identifying and affirming to realize that other people have thought the same thoughts, had the same struggles, felt the same longings.

Reading also provides a window on the world. Robert Lewis Stevenson wrote, "There is no frigate like a book," meaning books can take you to times and places you could never go in real life. I can read *Perelandra* and be on Venus or *Ben Hur* and be in the Roman Empire at the time of Christ or *Cold Sassy Tree* and feel what it was like to live in a small town in Georgia in the early 1900s. And rarely has there been a movie version that is as good as the original book, so watching movies based on books will not give you the feel, the language and the stimulation of imagination that comes from a good, well-written book.

From an educational point of view, being well-read places you in the small percentage of people who have a broader perspective of life—the movers and shakers of the world. Why? Because readers have superior language and thinking skills. They also know about life outside their narrow slice of it. They can see both the "big picture" and the details and keep a sense of perspective because they have read enough to expand their minds beyond the parameters of their own lives.

If books are to become an important part of your child's world, they must appear to be important to you. It is difficult to convince a child who never sees his or her parents with a book that reading is a pleasurable activity and that self-education is a worthwhile use of time.

Many parents lament that their daughters become avid readers, but their sons are totally disinterested. Our question to these parents is: Do your children ever see their father read? Boys who only see Mom read begin to associate reading with feminine activities.

Fathers we have posed this question to give all sorts of excuses for not reading—they don't have time, they are slow readers, they can't find anything they want to read, they don't like reading, and so on. If you are a father who doesn't enjoy personal reading, consider reading aloud to your children books that they enjoy. This way they can see you interacting with books, even if you don't read much yourself.

THE BENEFITS OF A PRINT RICH ENVIRONMENT

It has been proven that children who grow up in homes where they have access to lots of good books for them to read whenever they choose have naturally superior language art skills. A child who hears English properly used at home and consistently reads well-written literature will automatically internalize correct grammar, word usage, capitalization, punctuation, and spelling and will also develop an extensive vocabulary.

If that weren't enough to convince you that reading is one of the most important activities your child can do, *Cradles of Eminence* studied common factors in the childhoods of 400 eminent men and women and concluded: "A rule of thumb for predicting future success is to know the number of books in the home." With this in mind, you may want to slowly but surely build your own home library of proven favorites.

Although it may seem easier and cheaper to simply check books

---

A RULE OF THUMB FOR PREDICTING
FUTURE SUCCESS IS TO KNOW THE
NUMBER OF BOOKS IN THE HOME.

---

out from the library, children love to read and read and reread their favorites, and they take pleasure in having copies of books that have become their special friends. Also, if you have a large family, the books become an investment to be passed down to each succeeding child, and perhaps even to grandchildren.

WHAT DETERMINES IF A BOOK IS GOOD FOR CHILDREN?

There are three questions you can ask to determine if a book is good for children:

1 | *Has it stood the test of time?*

2 | *Is it well written?* Does the writer "talk down" to children, using jargon, modern language or a trite story line, or does he/she tell the tale well? C. S. Lewis said: "Any book worth reading at 10 should

be worth reading at 50."

3 | *Does it touch the heart in a positive way?* Does it reinforce noble desires or does it create longings that cannot be fulfilled in a godly way?

THE IMPORTANCE OF READING ALOUD TO YOUR CHILDREN

You will be amazed to discover that the simple act of reading aloud to your children is highly enjoyable, it deepens relationships, provides unique opportunities for sharing, and allows you access to their lives in ways few other activities can.

Reading aloud doesn't need to stop when the children can read. We read aloud together all during our children's schooling years, and I still read aloud on long car trips. I even read aloud with friends. We try to save books we want to discuss and read them aloud together, pausing whenever the book sparks an idea someone wants to comment on.

I even have adult friends who get together once a week and read a play. They switch around the roles and have a great time together.

Here are some suggestions for reading aloud gleaned from our own experience and from *The New Read Aloud Handbook* by Jim Trelease.

1 | Begin reading to children as soon as possible. Studies have shown that even reading to children in the womb enhances language recognition skills.

2 | Try and establish a routine time that children can anticipate and when reading can be leisurely and uninterrupted.

3 | Remember, the art of listening must be cultivated. Expect short attention spans at first. If you notice interest waning, read shorter selections or find books with short stories or chapters. However, if it is obvious that no one is interested in the book you've chosen, don't hesitate to put it aside and choose another.

4 | Start with picture books and gradually introduce stories and novels. Reword difficult passages. Vary the length, difficulty, and subject matter.

5 | Find a suspenseful spot at which to stop.

6 | Make sure everyone is comfortable.

7 | Allow time for discussion and meaningful interruptions, but don't turn discussions into quizzes, impose interpretations of the book's meaning on the listeners, or insist upon using the book as a teaching opportunity.

8 | Use plenty of expression, varying your tone of voice to fit the dialogue.

9 | Read slowly enough for the listeners to build mental pictures of what they have heard. Slow down in picture books and let children fully examine the illustrations.

10 | Add a third dimension to the book whenever possible, like serving blueberries when reading *Blueberries for Sal*.

11 | With boys, let the father do as much of the reading as possible.

12 | Allow children to color, play with legos, etc, especially for those who find it difficult to just sit and listen.

13 | Be aware of a child's maturity level and choose books that do not violate it. Many modern children's books contain illustrations or concepts that are inappropriate for a young child's level of emotional, mental, or spiritual maturity.

WHAT DO WE READ?

To help Christian parents choose the best in children's literature, the books below contain recommendations and annotated book lists.

The Read-Aloud Handbook by Jim Trelease. This book not only convinces you of the critical importance of reading aloud to your children, but it also has many lists of the "best of the best" books that all ages can read aloud and enjoy.

Invitation to the Classics by Louise Cowan and Os Guiness. Subtitled, "A Guide to the Books You Always Wanted to Read," the authors have prepared a history of literature by presenting, in chronological order, important literature in the history of Western civilization. This is a large, hardcover book for young adults and up.

Books Children Love by Elizabeth Wilson is a wonderful book derived from the insights of Charlotte Mason who believed education should take place mainly through reading books that make a subject come alive. It lists hundreds of "living books" by subject area and grade level from preschool through eighth grade.

Books by Gladys Hunt: *Honey for a Child's Heart* gives many suggestions for making reading more rewarding and includes an 85 page annotated booklist of the best children's literature by subject and age level. *Honey for a Teen's Heart* is the sequel to *Honey for a Child's Heart* and has teen reading lists and lots of ideas for creating teen readers and keeping them reading. *Honey for a Woman's Heart* is another great reading compilation, this time for busy Christian women.

Reading Lists for College Bound Students contains suggested reading lists from 100 top colleges, an annotated list of the 100 books colleges most often recommend, and suggestions for planning a high school reading program. (See also the S.A.T.s recommended reading list for college bound students.)

This chapter was written by Ellyn Davis and is excerpted from the e-book **Teaching Language Arts at Home** *available at www.homeschoolmarketplace.com. On the Home School Marketplace website we recommend many books that are proven favorites with children and are considered great children's literature.*

15

MY CHILDREN AND I HAVE READ countless books together and people often say to me, "Well, it's fine to read all those books with your children, but how do you find the time?" Reading great books must be our first educational priority. Let the textbooks and workbooks take second or even third place. I believe that the education of home school children would be enhanced if an entire school year were taken off to focus on reading excellent literature.

When I was pregnant with my fifth child, I had an opportunity to test this theory. It was not by choice, but by necessity, that we implemented this mode of learning.

I was sick almost the entire pregnancy and spent much of the time in bed. (One of my sons relates now that all of his memories of me during that period are horizontal!) The children gathered in my bed and listened to me read aloud for hours, though I admit, I worried that they might suffer academically. The opposite proved to be true as I observed that their vocabulary, thinking, and composition skills soared.

When it was time for annual testing, their reading, spelling, and math scores had actually improved. This was enough proof for me: exposure to great literature stimulates the mind. Since that time, literature has held a high position in our home.

CHILDREN REFLECT THEIR PARENTS' INTEREST IN READING

It is whether we, as parents, value reading that determines whether our children will be attracted to reading. Parental involvement and absorption in reading relates directly to the child's ability and desire to learn to read. In other words, the more involved the parent is, the more interested the child will be.

My strong belief in the value of sharing great literature with my children is confirmed again and again as I study the works of educators such as Ruth Beechick, Charlotte Mason, and Susan Schaeffer MacCaulay.

Reading widely not only helps to stimulate our children's academic abilities, but it stimulates their creative abilities as well. Sharing great books with our children—books teaming with life—provides an avenue for creative activity. Reading these books together allows us to spend precious time with our children while strengthening their academic and creative skills.

A good book will transport us to another place and time and help us to become intimately acquainted with great individuals—real heroes and heroines. A biography offers us an opportunity to tread in another person's footsteps, enabling us to share in their triumph, defeat, anguish, and jubilation. Even a well-crafted fictional character may offer us a glimpse of true heroism.

I treasure memories of my children acting out characters from classics such as *Pilgrim's Progress, Heidi, Swiss Family Robinson*, and *The Secret Garden*. The majority of children today spend more time watching TV and videos than they do absorbing good literature. They are generally held hostage by the cookie cutter heroes (pressed out of an inferior mold) formed by the latest TV or movie craze.

One cannot walk down the aisle of a store without being bombarded by this mediocrity. I think over-stimulation from the media has squelched our children's natural inquisitiveness so they settle for the mundane and the mediocre. I will grant some videos and TV programs have good things to offer and are not to be discounted entirely. However, we should not allow the good things to crowd out the best things.

CHILDREN ENJOY LITERATURE FROM AN EARLY AGE

Follow a plan of reading aloud that introduces new levels of difficulty as the child develops. Begin with picture books for young children. Bright pictures focus the child's attention while still leaving much to

---

READING GREAT BOOKS MUST BE OUR FIRST EDUCATIONAL PRIORITY. LET THE TEXTBOOKS AND WORKBOOKS TAKE SECOND OR EVEN THIRD PLACE. I BELIEVE THAT THE EDUCATION OF HOME SCHOOL CHILDREN WOULD BE ENHANCED IF AN ENTIRE SCHOOL YEAR WERE TAKEN OFF TO FOCUS ON READING EXCELLENT LITERATURE.

---

the imagination—more so than videos, which bombard them with fast moving pictures and sounds.

Picture books also help young children develop an appreciation for art while building familiarity with the rhythm and flow of our language. As children mature they will enjoy other types of books: fantasy, fiction, non-fiction, poetry, biographies, and more.

My children have learned to enjoy literature from an early age. It is exciting for me to see that literature continues to hold a place of high importance for my teenagers. Recently, my 17-year-old daughter, Melissa, said to me, "One of my goals in life is to read all of the classics. I think I have a pretty good start so far." We then discussed our favorite authors and books, and she commented, "I'm interested in reading books that were written at least a hundred years ago. Most of the books that are being written today can't compare with these, so why waste my time?"

Years of learning alongside my children have taught me the value of reading great books with them. By "great books," I mean books that stimulate the mind and arouse the heart. Great books help us to grow intellectually and spiritually. They allow us to experience loyalty, courage, honesty, truth, wisdom, and other enduring qualities through the creative expression of the author. Great books are of outstanding literary quality.

I wish that I had realized the importance of reading literature with my children earlier in my home schooling experience. It is so easy to be caught up in completing this textbook or that workbook to the point that meaningful education is pushed aside. Reading great books with our children has provided us with many wonderful educational experiences, and reading aloud to them from an early age has prepared them to begin formal reading instruction.

THE POSITIVE INFLUENCE OF LITERATURE

As my children play I am reminded of the positive influence of literature in their lives. When my youngest daughter, Mandy was 7 years old, she began taking piano lessons. This sparked an interest in the lives of the great composers, so we read more than twenty biographies. Some were the easy-reader-type, which she could read to me, while others were more lengthy books, which I read to her. I was amazed at how she kept the events of the different composer's lives so neatly sorted.

This enthusiasm flowed over into her playtime where she centered her activities on a composer's era. She managed to draw her 3-year-old brother, Randall, into her pretend world. I recall one day in particular when they were totally absorbed in their play. I rushed into the bedroom because we were hurrying to leave for an appointment, and there they stood—coats on (in the heat of summer) and suitcases in hand. I abruptly commanded, "Hurry up! We are going to be late for the orthodontist. Take off these things, and get into the van."

Mandy and Randall took no notice of me. I repeated my orders. Then Mandy said, in an emphatic tone, "He's Mozart and I'm Nannerl,

---

YEARS OF LEARNING ALONGSIDE MY CHILDREN HAVE TAUGHT ME THE VALUE OF READING GREAT BOOKS WITH THEM.

Mozart's sister. Mozart's performing at a concert tonight in Vienna. We must be off to Vienna at once!"

"I'm sorry," I said. "Mozart can have his concert when we come back home. We must go to the orthodontist now."

My teenage son, Robert, was listening from the hallway. He burst into the bedroom, exclaiming, "Nannerl, Mozart, we must hurry! The last coach leaves for Vienna in five minutes!"

Without a word, the two little waifs, with coats on and suitcases in hand, ran outside and jumped into the van. I stood silently in the bedroom for a few moments, until my son put his hand on my shoulder and said, "Mom, you just have to meet them in their world."

I encourage you to assist your children in creating worlds of their own. A great book is a gateway into such golden worlds.

P.S. I have always relied on *Honey for a Child's Heart*, *Books Children Love*, and *Honey for a Teen's Heart*.

This chapter was written by Valerie Bendt. Valerie and her husband, Bruce have home schooled their six children for over 25 years. She has written the following books for home schoolers: **How to Create Your Own Unit Study, The Unit Study Idea Book, For the Love of Reading,** *and* **Success with Unit Studies.** *She has also written* **The Frances Study Guide, Creating Books with Children, Successful Puppet Making, Making the Most of the Preschool Years,** *and* **Reading Made Easy.** *Valerie is a popular conference speaker. Visit www.homeschoolmarketplace.com for a list of Valerie Bendt's recommended books for children as well as book lists for all ages from preschool through high school.*

16

TEACHING MATH

AS A HOMESCHOOL MOM with a math education background, I am seen as the answer person for homeschool math questions, such as:

What is the best math curriculum?
When do I need to start teaching math?
Do I need to drill the times tables?
How much math do I need to teach?

Because I love math, it is my favorite subject to teach. My passion has caused me to develop some opinions about how to teach it. I do not claim to be a math education expert. My opinions come from twenty-one years of homeschooling four children, from my interactions with other homeschoolers and from my own study.

One of the reasons I chose to homeschool was that it provided me the freedom to tailor the education of my children around their unique interests and abilities as well as the family's priorities. I didn't want to do it the way the school did it; I wanted to do it differently and better. When homeschooling parents adopt the institutional approach to education, they miss out on so many of the beauties of homeschooling. If you are going to homeschool, take advantage of its many benefits. Three of the goals I had for my homeschool were that my children would love to learn, know how to learn, and be allowed to learn at their own pace. I saw many problems that were caused by children being pushed to do something before they were developmentally ready. We often see children pushed in reading, but it also happens with math.

MATH AND THE YOUNG CHILD

In her book titled *An Easy Start In Arithmetic*, Ruth Beechick says there are three modes in which children think about math: manipulative, mental and abstract. These modes also correspond to the developmental stages of a child. First, young children learn through the manipulative stage. They need to see, touch, feel and move objects. When you, as an adult, see the problem 2+3=5, you think in the abstract mode. You understand the concept of two and three. You do not have to see and touch two blocks and three blocks. You don't even have to picture two blocks and three blocks in your head. Preschoolers cannot think abstractly; they are in the manipulative stage. They need the blocks in their hands because they can't yet imagine them in their heads.

Later, during elementary school, children develop the ability to do math in the mental mode. They can picture the number and the addition process, but they are still not able to understand the abstract concept of a number. This ability to understand the abstract concepts of math develops around age twelve.

It's best for a homeschooling parent to keep these developmental stages in mind while teaching math. During the early years, math concepts need to be taught with things that the child can see, touch, feel and manipulate. This need usually corresponds nicely with the real life of the child. Children need a lot of real-world, concrete experiences before they can internalize the meaning of numbers, arithmetic operations, geometric shapes, proportion and all the other terms, ideas, processes and relationships that are a part of mathematics.

One of the best things homeschool parents can do is to get a good elementary math book and read it themselves. Learn the terms and concepts, and then apply these terms and concepts to your child's everyday life. Many homeschool parents hate math and do not feel very competent to teach it. If this is true of you, you need to do some homework. The more you understand the concepts yourself, the better off your children will be. Now I'm not talking about algebra; I'm

---

I WANT TO PREPARE MY CHILDREN TO BE ABLE TO DO WHATEVER THEY ARE CALLED TO DO. EVEN IF THEY ARE NOT CALLED TO DO ANYTHING MATHEMATICAL, THEY MAY BE CALLED TO DO SOMETHING THAT REQUIRES COLLEGE, AND COLLEGE REQUIRES THREE TO FOUR YEARS OF HIGH SCHOOL MATH.

---

talking about early elementary math.

Children come into contact with math everyday. When children play with building blocks, puzzles, toy cars, when they have a need for counting, patterning, comparing, estimating, etc., they are building a repertoire of concrete experience. Helping mom in the kitchen or dad in the workshop offers many opportunities for real-life math. Gardening, playing a musical instrument, grocery shopping, setting the table, and playing board games are all examples of activities that provide children with context and a frame of reference for future math learning.

It is so important that your children have these experiences before they start a formal math program. I actually don't start a formal program until third grade. Until that time, I do real-life math, read math books, do math activities and play math while occasionally throwing in a few math lessons. A book that is fun to use during the elementary ages is *Family Math*. Also, the library is full of picture books with a mathematical theme.

Once a child has the developmental maturity of a third grader, he is able to cover K through second grade math rather quickly and can then move on to third grade math. You could probably wait a little longer, if you're patient and have the nerve to stand up against peer pressure. A student who has had a life rich in mathematical experiences will be better able to understand the math exercises that he is now asked to do. During this stage, he is able to do mental math. He doesn't always need the manipulatives because he is able to picture them in his head. Manipulatives are sometimes helpful, especially when learning a new or difficult concept or process. However, be careful that you don't expect him to be able to do the abstract thinking that is required for many math processes. He is not ready for that yet.

FLEXIBILITY

Flexibility is one of the greatest advantages of homeschooling. Your child can move as quickly or as slowly as necessary. If your child is getting the material quickly and seems bored or frustrated with doing all of the problems, then cut out some of the problems and move on. You have an advantage over the classroom teacher of knowing your student very well. You will be able to determine whether he is getting it or not. If he is having difficulty, then slow down, or take a break and come back a few weeks later. If you decide it is time to take a break from progressing in math, don't just stop doing math altogether.

I know you have heard the expression, "If you don't use it, you lose it." This is especially true of math. Keep doing review even when you are taking a break from introducing new material.

My oldest daughter, who is now a college graduate with degrees in math and music, was always good at math. I could tell from early on that she was gifted in this area. When she was going into the third grade, I started her in a sixth grade math book and spent two years in the book. Because this book started with so much review we were able to start in this book without having to do very much outside review. This worked, in a way. She did well academically, but she hated math. This bad attitude was a major red flag for me. One of my goals was for my children to have a good attitude about learning. I had to do something to fix this problem, especially since I knew she was gifted in this area. So, we took the next year off from progressing in math. I did consistent review for this year. However, the review did not take much time, so it really was a break. When she came back to learning math during the sixth grade, she had a much better attitude. (I need to add here that it was *MathCounts*, a math problem solving and competition club for junior high students that turned her into a math lover.)

I tell you this story to show an example of the creativity you can have in the homeschool environment. You are not locked into the traditional program of conquering a new math book each year and staying on grade level. Also, don't feel that you have to use the same curriculum every year. You can alternate or switch books if you don't like the one you are using. Different programs work better for different kids.

I also recommend that you do math along with your student when at all possible, especially if this is a first child. It will help you review the math concepts, and is also good for your student to work closely with you. Remember that your attitude about a subject is more important than your knowledge about it. I remember pretending to be fascinated with the discovery of bugs and snakes when my children were little. If I can do this, you can pretend to like math. You don't have to pretend to be good at it, though. It is good for your child to see you learning with him.

I am often asked about memorizing math facts such as the times table. I take a middle of the road approach on this topic. While I do think it is important that children know the math facts, I do not agree with stopping everything else until they are memorized. I usually took some time to work on memorizing the facts, and then I moved on before they were perfected. I found the more math the student did, the more these facts became a part of his knowledge. So I used a combination of some work on memorizing the facts and a lot of work on using them.

PROBLEM SOLVING SKILLS

I usually teach problem solving skills while my children are doing their final years of elementary math and along with algebra. Many people tend to ignore these skills because they are not covered well in most textbooks, and covering them takes extra time and resources.

One reason I take two years to cover Algebra 1 is to have the student work on problem solving. In real life, math problems do not come with a label. You have to figure out what kind of problem it is and then how to solve that problem. Textbooks usually have exercises after a lesson is taught. The student exercises the skills that he has just learned by doing the exercises. Problem solving, on the other hand, teaches the student to look at a problem and determine what kind of problem it is and how it should be solved. This skill is much more helpful in real-life than the ability to work exercises at the end of a lesson. The textbook exercises provide skills and knowledge that are necessary for solving problems. The *MathCounts* competition is very effective in teaching problem solving skills. These skills will help your student in all areas of math, and it is great preparation for the SAT. This competition for seventh and eighth grade is especially good for children who are good at math. It is a challenging program, however, and can be discouraging for those who are weak in math.

Another math problem solving program is the *Math Olympiad* program. It is a problem solving competition for grades four through eight. The book, *Math Olympiad Contest Problems for Elementary and Middle Schools* by George Lenchner is a great supplement to your math curriculum. This book is also a good choice for junior high students who find *MathCounts* too difficult. I use the *Math Olympiad* book (it is an easy book to use) during the last couple of years of elementary math as a supplement, and the students love it. I remember one student who hated math before she started doing *Math Olympiad* problems stating, "Math is so cool!" after just two days of doing these problems. I never participated in the *Math Olympiad* competitions, but they are available.

BEYOND ELEMENTARY MATH

Once elementary math is conquered, its time for Algebra. I usually take two years to do Algebra

It is important that the student have a good understanding of Algebra because it is the foundation of the rest of math. Don't rush it, and don't move on until each concept is grasped. I absolutely love *Elementary Algebra* by Harold Jacobs. The more I use it, the more I like it. I also like *Jacobs Geometry*.

Many people have difficulty in seeing the practical application of teaching the higher levels of math. They don't see that they use algebra in their daily lives, so they wonder why they need to learn it or teach it. I am convinced that higher levels of math teach us to think more clearly and logically. How important is this to your daily life? The process of thinking that is taught in algebra and geometry teaches us to process information in a logical way. Other than my love for math and the connection with thinking skills, I do have other reasons for having my children learn higher math. I want to prepare my children to be able to do whatever they are called to do. Even if they are not called to do anything mathematical, they may be called to do something that requires college, and college requires three to four years of high school math. Until my children reach high school, I homeschool them the way I want. We study what we want, how we want, and when we want. When they get to high school, I make some compromises to prepare them for college. I make sure that they have two years of foreign language and three years of science, whether I feel that they need it for their life or not.

Now, I don't completely cave in to the traditionalists. I do a lot of things in a homeschooly way. I integrate many of the subjects, emphasize math and science for those students with that bent, and emphasize history and government for the students with that bent. My children with a musical gift are active in music activities while the future politician will be in debate. So each student's high school experience will be different.

Earlier I mentioned that many people don't think that algebra and geometry are needed for everyday life. I don't believe that this is true. Because I am comfortable with this knowledge of math, I do occasionally find myself using this information to solve real-life problems. Also, if your children end up being homeschool parents, it will be very helpful for them to know these subjects.

To sum up the reasons why I think higher level math is important:

- It teaches logical thinking.

- It prepares a student for his potential calling.

- It prepares a student for college.

- It teaches math skills that may be needed for real-life.

- It prepares future parents to pass along important math skills to the next generation.

Being a math major with a love of math, I place a high priority on learning math. However, I realize that not all homeschoolers share the same priorities. Each homeschooling family brings its own set of priorities to the homeschooling situation. God knows this when he places children in families. He knew that I would place a priority on math and not on foreign language, for example. So, I will take all of my children at least through pre-calculus. However, it is hard to say what level of math is right for every student. Each student is different and has a different calling on his life. We as parents need to study each child, praying for wisdom in planning each one's education. As we pray and plan, God will lead us to make the right decisions for each child. He knows the plans He has for each of them.

This chapter was written by Debbie Mason. Debbie and her husband Spencer live in North Carolina and Debbie has homeschooled all four of her children as well as been a statewide homeschooling leader in North Carolina.

17

TEACHING HISTORY: IMPARTING PERSPECTIVE

THE FOUNDATION OF OUR HISTORY STUDY is *The Narrated Bible* (paperback version called the *Daily Bible*). This is a NIV translation arranged in chronological order. *The Child's Story Bible* is another help, because it sets the stage historically for each of the Bible stories. As we follow the biblical account, we branch off into different historical periods as we come to them. Once we finish the Bible, history study can be continued by correlating the different time periods with church history. *Sketches From Church History* is an excellent interdenominational view of church history that clearly explains the effect of Christianity on different nations of the world. Another wonderful history source is *Streams of Civilization*. It correlates the study of world history with the study of the Bible and church history.

Studying history as we read through the Bible allows us to leisurely study different time periods. We don't have to cram 4000 years of history into one year. We can spend weeks on Egypt as we read about Joseph and Moses, or spend months on the Roman Empire as we work through the New Testament. Another benefit of this approach is that all the children can study the same historical period at the same time, each at his or her own level.

Don't feel that you have to teach history chronologically, however. Since young children don't have the big picture anyway and they are constantly receiving information about different time periods from the world around them, you can pluck out any time period on which you want to focus. In our home, we feel free to modify our overall study of history when opportunities arise to have a first-hand encounter with a historical site. One spring we went to a book fair in Boston and visited Plimoth Plantation, Ellis Island, and the Statue of Liberty on the way home. We would have been foolish to stolidly stick to a chronological study of history when we had an opportunity to let the children learn about the Pilgrims in the 1600s and the wave of immigration in the late 1800s by actually being where it all happened. The children don't get confused as to where these events fit into the scheme of history if we use a time line. Studying history through travel makes a time period "come alive" in a way that books cannot do.

HOW TO STUDY HISTORY

If you like the idea of leisurely following history chronologically, then the beginning is a great place to start, and the Bible is the best textbook. The biblical events in Genesis and the first part of Exodus flow very naturally through the period of early mankind. We read aloud from the *Narrated Bible*. Most children will understand the NIV version when it is read aloud and difficult words are explained. Maps can be just as important a visual aid as a timeline. A good Bible mapbook is a must when studying the Bible. Another helpful book for this early period of history is *Adam and His Kin* by Ruth Beechick. *Streams of Civilization* uses the Biblical method of historical interpretation starting with creation and is perfect as a core of world history before 1600.

Where do you go from there? After children have a firm grasp of the foundations of history (creation, the fall, God's call, the patriarchs), when you get to the story of Joseph in the Bible you can move into a study of ancient Egypt.

At this point you may continue to use *Streams of Civilization* and supplemental reading such as Usborne books and historical fiction or start with Greenleaf Press' history series. *The Greenleaf Guide to Ancient Egypt* organizes a course of study based on the first four books of the Bible that integrates activities, Usborne books, biographies, and historical fiction. The Greenleaf Guide is adaptable and can be used with children of various ages.

Another option is the Usborne books. Children love to study history with Usborne's colorful illustrations. In short, visual chapters each book provides the bare bones of the major developments of the world. The books look at individual civilizations and vividly describe how people lived, their discoveries and inventions, their conflicts with rival civilizations, and their contributions to our own cultural heritage. *The Usborne Book of World History* gives a chronological pictorial history of the world on an elementary to junior high level.

What about biographies and historical fiction?

Emerson said "There is no history, only biography." History is essentially the study of people, what they did, and why they did it. While studying a time period, a wonderful way to get a feel for that period is to read about someone who lived through it.

There are many wonderful books about interesting people in history. These books secure attention, interest, and concentration with little teaching effort. Good historical fiction can also make a period of time "come alive" and provide a fascinating window into the past.

What if I can't do a chronological study of history?

Studying history chronologically from creation to modern times may not work for you. We have alternated our study of world history with U.S. history, studying one time period at a time. Once you get a timeline going, you will be able to place the periods of time in a chronological sequence so that your children can grasp the overall picture.

In teaching history, as in teaching science, we believe that the elementary grades should be used to lay a broad foundation and generate enthusiasm. We recommend that you read the chapters on teaching history in Ruth Beechick's *You CAN Teach Your Child Successfully* and Valerie Bendt's *How to Create Your Own Unit Study*. They share a wealth of ideas for creating a broad foundation and promoting a lifelong

---

IN TEACHING HISTORY AS IN TEACHING SCIENCE, WE BELIEVE THAT THE ELEMENTARY GRADES SHOULD BE USED TO LAY A BROAD FOUNDATION AND GENERATE ENTHUSIASM.

---

interest in history. Kathryn Stout's *Guides to History* gives detailed information on creating a unit study around a historic period, event, people, or culture.

TEACHING HISTORY IN THE ELEMENTARY GRADES

There are two theories about how to teach history to elementary aged children. One theory is to start with the familiar and move to the less familiar. This theory is the one used in American public schools. With this approach to history the child first learns about his own community ("The fireman is our friend," and other "community awareness" topics), then about his state, and then about his country. If you look at public school scope and sequence charts, children usually are studying some form of American history every single year from first through seventh grade. World History is often only a one year course in tenth or eleventh grade. This same format is also used in several of the textbook curricula available for home schoolers.

The second theory about teaching history to elementaries is that children need to be exposed to world history at a young age as a prelude to understanding the history of America as well as to understand Bible stories. Greenleaf Press and Beautiful Feet Books have taken this approach to history and their materials provide elementary aged children with a chronological study of history from ancient times to the present. We tend to think there needs to be a little of both: children should have a grasp of both where we came from (World History) and where we are now (American History), and whatever materials you use to accomplish that are the ones that should be followed.

In the primary years (approximately grades K - 3) children need to develop the concepts of past, present, and future, and to understand that people lived before everyone they know was born and that those people had different ways of doing things. This can easily be accomplished through reading a wide variety of good historical children's literature. Young children best understand history as stories of "once upon a time" or "long ago," and are particularly interested in tales of what their own family did in the past. For this reason we have made an effort to trace our genealogy back as far as possible and to collect family stories. We also read aloud a lot of Bible stories and books that expose the children to different time periods and different cultures.

At about 4th or 5th grade children reach the information stage of reading where they can actually learn from what they read themselves. At this point they can begin a more earnest study of history. However, they still need the story approach as much as possible because they have little understanding of chronology, of the political and economic motivations of adults, or of the sinfulness of man. This is why "story-centered" history programs such as the Greenleaf Guides and the Beautiful Feet books are so successful. At this age, we try to provide a general framework of the main historical periods. This framework can be filled in with details later. It's like giving the plot outline, main characters, and interesting highlights of a play and waiting until the children are older to fill in all the details of the staging and action. This is also the time to reinforce the concept that all history is really "His" story. Time on earth can be divided into the following periods: God's Creation, Man's Fall, The Promise of Jesus, Jesus Comes, and Preparation for Jesus to come Again. Each of those periods can be subdivided. For example, Preparation for Jesus to Come Again includes The Early Church, The Middle Ages, The Renaissance and Reformation, Rise of World Powers, and The Modern World.

One thing you could ask yourself (and your children) is why the Bible and historians give such different emphases to different peoples, cultures and time periods. The Bible ignores individuals and cultures which historians consider important, and vice versa.

TEACHING HISTORY TO JUNIOR HIGH AND HIGH SCHOOL AGES

At around 7th to 9th grade, children are ready to be challenged with thinking about problems of mankind, comparing world views, and the ideologies behind historical events. They can begin reading more mature books and pursue in-depth study of historical periods. From this point on, textbooks may be helpful but should not be overused. For example, a study of the French Revolution could include reading *A Tale of Two Cities* and *The Scarlet Pimpernel* with the textbook used as a reference to fill in the gaps. Use Schaeffer's *How Should We Then Live?* as an accompaniment to provoke deeper questions such as: "Why was the French Revolution so different from the American Revolution when they were founded on many of the same ideals and occurred within 25 years of each other?"

This is also a good age for children to begin making their own "Book of Centuries" which is a time line in book form that the child assembles himself, with each page representing 100 years. For each century, the child enters written information, illustrations, brief bio-graphical sketches of major figures, etc. The result is a combination time line and historical scrapbook. This is a very effective way to study history. A Book of Centuries may be hand-made, but ready-made ones are available.

The Kingfisher History Encyclopedia (which is really a history text) does an outstanding job of explaining and illustrating the ten differ-ent historical time periods: The Ancient World (from prehistory to the founding of Rome), The Classical World (Greece and Rome), The Early Middle Ages (from the fall of Rome to around 1100), The Middle Ages, The Renaissance and Reformation, Trade and Empire (1600s), Revolution and Independence (1700s and 1800s), Unification and Colonization (mid-1800s to World War I), The World at War (1914 - 1949), and Modern Times (1950 to the present). Whereas the elementary years were concerned with establishing mental images of each period and with learning some of the more important names and events, the high school years are concerned with "fleshing out" the mental images, learning even more important names and events, and, most of all, with beginning to understand some of the "why" of history. Older students are ready to grasp the ideas that led people to make discoveries, invent things, wage war, and keep peace.

At the high school level, most states require one credit of World History and Geography, one credit of American History and Geography, one credit of American Government, and two to three credits of "Social Studies," which can be more World History, American History, Geography, or Government, or it can be other courses such as Anthropology, Philosophy, Sociology, Economics, Career Choices, or Biblical History. High School is when we can take a serious look at what each child's future holds and whether that future includes study or a career that needs a lot of history. Some careers, such as lawyer, teacher, archaeologist, anthropologist, or economist, require more history than others. Also, some children are deeply interested in history. Let the child's desires and future needs determine the amount of history study. Another option for the high school years is to focus on passing the CLEP tests or Advanced Placement Tests in history so freshman and sophomore history classes in college can be exempted.

APPROACHES TO WORLD HISTORY

History teaching materials usually take one of several approaches to history (or a combination):

The Events Approach:

What happened? History is seen as a succession of events with turning points of wars, inventions, and discoveries. The old PBS series "The Day the Universe Changed" and "Connections" were prime examples of taking an event (such as the development of the printing press) and following its impact on the course of history. Just learning names, dates, and events is guaranteed to make history boring, but *The Events Approach* can be very effective if children are presented with high-interest highlights of history (such as the Usborne books), with "stories" (good historical fiction as in the Beautiful Feet guides), or with an unusual twist (such as the PBS series).

The People Approach:

Who made it happen? History is learned by studying the people who made it. In this approach, history is seen as a succession of real stories about real people. Biographies are studied as well as good historical fiction. This is a very effective approach with elementary and junior high students. Good examples of this approach are the books by Greenleaf Press (*Famous Men* and *Guides to Famous Men*).

The Ideas Approach:

Why did it happen? Older students are ready to grasp the ideas that led people to make discoveries, invent things, wage war, and keep peace. Behind every person and event in history was an ideology, a world view, a way of looking at and living life. The WHY of history can be studied in three ways: (1) from the biblical point of view that God raises up people and nations as instruments for the chastening of His people and for the sake of the spread of the Gospel; (2) by examining biblical principles either adhered to or violated and the resulting consequences for a person or nation; and/or (3) by analyzing the influence of various ways of thinking on the course of civilization.

The Geographical Approach:

Where did it happen? Much of history has to do with the lay of the land. It is always wise to study geography along with history because then you can see why events followed certain routes.

STUDYING AMERICAN HISTORY

Since America was founded upon a Reformation base, it is easy to go from a study of the Renaissance and Reformation directly into American history. In fact, some history programs consider the signing of the Magna Carta in 1215 the pivotal event leading to our democratic republic, and their materials for American history begin at that date. (See products from Beautiful Feet, *America's Providential History*, and *The Story of Liberty*.)

Materials for studying American history assume the same approaches as materials available for world history, but there is a distinct difference. The difference is that America is the only nation founded upon a base of Reformation Christianity. Our founding fathers, although not all Christian, operated out of a Christian consensus of moral belief, appealed to the power of prayer, and recognized God's intervention on our behalf at certain crisis periods in our history. Our governmental system reflects its framers' belief in biblical law and politics. Our history is, to a great degree, Christian history.

MAKE A CONCERTED EFFORT TO DECIDE WHAT IT IS ABOUT HISTORY THAT REALLY MATTERS TO YOU AND FOCUS ON THAT WITH YOUR CHILDREN.

Modern secular textbooks omit references to the Christian origins of our nation and distort events in such a way as to discredit God's influence over them. Christian historians have tried to make Christians aware of these omissions and distortions. *Teaching and Learning America's Christian History* by J. Stephen Wilkins is an excellent audio set that discusses the importance of studying history ("A nation deceived about its past can be easily manipulated in the present."); the Christian perspective of history; how we can study American history; and what we can do to pass on the knowledge of what God has done for us in the past. Peter Marshall also has a series of books on America's Christian history beginning with *The Light and the Glory*.

USING TRAVEL TO STUDY HISTORY

We were fortunate, because our family business required us to travel all across the United States while our boys were growing up, so we made sure we turned our business travels into opportunities for history study.

At various times we traveled across the country on the Oregon Trail starting in St. Louis at the Museum of Westward Expansion; we followed the Sante Fe and Chisolm Trails through the southwestern United States; we drove up the eastern seaboard visiting colonial and Revolutionary War sites; we studied the southern states by traveling to Civil War battle sites; and we followed the Underground Railroad from Tennessee to Ohio. We made each of these trips opportunities to study the history, geography, flora and fauna of the areas we were visiting, so our children got a real understanding of the progression of American history as well as of U.S. geography and ecology.

We've also taken family trips or mission trips overseas to Israel where we studied biblical history; to France where we studied World War II and visited the D-Day landing sites; to Great Britian; and to Africa.

You may not have opportunities to travel on this same scale, but there is no reason you can't plan camping trips or family vacations around historical study. You can also take part in re-inactments. Some of our homeschooling friends participate in Civil War battle reinactments and even appeared in the movie *Gettysburg*. There are also reinactments of battles from other historical time periods that you and your children can enjoy either as spectators or participants.

Using Time Lines

Using a time line is one of the most effective ways to help children develop a concept of history.

However, a time line will not pull together a child's scattered pieces of knowledge like it does for adults. Children haven't collected enough pieces to pull together. What time lines *can* do is function as "pegboards" where children hang bits of historical information as they learn them. For this purpose a time line should be very simple, simple enough to memorize the major time periods. A simple Bible time line would be: Creation, Fall, Flood, Babel, Patriarchs, Egypt and Wilderness, Conquest, Judges, Kings, Captivity and Return, Jesus, Early Church, and Future Events.

Avoid cluttering a time line. The temptation is to divide each period into subheadings like arts, sciences, leaders, etc. and to have hundreds of little bits of information for each time frame. This may be helpful for young adults, but it's confusing to elementary and intermediate children.

Stick to the main events and people that characterize or "bring to life" that particular period. You will find it very helpful to read the chapter on teaching history in *You CAN Teach Your Child Successfully* and the recommendations for what children should know about history in *Teaching Children*. Unless your child shows a definite bent toward being a historian, don't overburden him with more than he needs to know. Make history interesting, not a facts-gathering marathon.

USING STORY TELLING

When our children were young we would often tell bedtime stories with our boys as the main characters, going back in time and meeting Bible personalities or famous historical figures good and bad. In these stories the boys would help, encourage, warn, face danger, make mistakes, sometimes even sin and repent. These were their favorite story times and it kept us thinking up new ways to get them into the past and back home again.

Genealogical research to dig up family stories is also a very effective teaching tool because you can study the historical period along with the stories about your own ancestors.

How Much Is Enough?

Make a concerted effort to decide what it is about history that really matters to you and will really matter to your children and focus on that as you teach your children. If you are someone who simply loves history, you will probably be able to transfer that love to your children unless you spoil things by using too much "book learning."

It is my opinion that the study of history is essential and the next chapter by Carole Joy Seid will emphasize this point. I think a person needs to know such things as what the word "Renaissance" means when he or she reads it in a book or hears it in a conversation. And, what does "Middle Ages" mean? What was it the "middle" of? Why were the "Dark Ages" dark? And were they really dark?

Most influential historians agree that the nature of man has not changed throughout history and that man will act pretty much as he has acted in the past, given the same set of circumstances today. This fact alone makes the study of history important because to know what to expect from man in certain circumstances is to have a ready response in one's present generation.

There are many things that move the course of humanity, but ideas have the most lasting affect by far. Because of that, the most effective study of history is from the perspective of the ideas that caused men and women to act as they did during various historical periods.

This chapter was written by Ellyn Davis. The Home School Marketplace website has lists of great children's historical literature for each different time period in U.S. and World History.

18

TEACHING HISTORY THROUGH LITERATURE

IN THE EARLY YEARS OF BEING a home schooling parent, when my son J.J. was a little boy, I would go to curriculum fairs and spend tons of money on tons of things that I took home and never used. It became a very expensive habit. As the years passed and I kept spending money for things that sat on my shelf, I began to ask myself, "Why do I keep buying this stuff?" I never felt comfortable using it, and after a week or two of enthusiasm and exhaustion it would wind up in a closet somewhere. It took a while, but I finally realized that I really didn't want someone telling me I had to do 30 minutes of geography on Tuesday morning at 10 o'clock and an hour of science on Friday at noon. On the other hand, I had friends who had their kids playing educational computer games all day long, and their attitude was, "Oh, well! It's getting the job done and it's good for their hand-eye coordination." Other friends had their kids plunked down on the couch in front of teaching videos all day. I knew that these methods were definitely not my style either, so I kept looking for my niche. What was my style of teaching and what felt right for me? What could I get up every morning and be enthusiastic about? What would work best for my son?

Over the course of several years, it gradually dawned on me that history is the logical core of all the rest of the curriculum. That is, if you want to build your own curriculum, history is the simplest, most common sense framework to build it on. History makes a great framework for all the other subjects because it follows a progression and covers everything else (except maybe math) like art, music, science, literature, and so on.

The other reason I decided history would make a good core curriculum was that as a school teacher, both in public and Christian schools, I saw that our children are "American Historied" to death. The longer I taught and the longer I studied history myself, the more I realized that most children think the world began in 1492. They picture the history of humanity a lot like those gag maps you can buy that show the United States taking up most of the world, with just a little room left over for some of the other nations, like Mexico and Canada to squeeze on the map. If they study history at all in school (which is unlikely, because schools seldom teach history anymore—they teach social studies instead), children would normally cover 300 years of history in eleven years of school, and 4000 years of history in one year of school. I don't know about you, but I think that is a little unbalanced.

Not only is that approach unbalanced, but it robs our children of a true understanding of why the world is like it is today. I strongly believe that as a Christian parent one of my responsibilities is to help my children develop a Christian worldview—a warp and woof that they see the world through so that when they read a book, see a movie, hear a song, go to a play, or whatever, they can discern the worldview being presented. The only way that discernment can be fully developed is to teach children about Western civilization and lay a foundation historically and philosophically from the time they are very young.

Even if our goal is to have our children love America and know American history, they cannot truly understand American history and thought without having some foundational understanding of the history of Israel, Greece, Rome, and Europe. After all, where do we think the founding fathers got their ideas about how a nation should be governed, about the rights of men, about law and justice? Do we think, "Poof!" they came out of a cloud somewhere? No, it didn't happen that way. Our culture and country were birthed out of a long history of government and thought over the past four to five thousand years. So, if you want to study American history, that's great. But study it chronologically where it belongs, which is at the end of 4000 plus years of civilization.

Now, how do we go about making history the backbone of our curriculum?

RECOMMENDATIONS FOR THE EARLY YEARS

I prefer not to jump into a time line and start serious historical study until children are about third grade. If a child is too young, a lot of history can be too abstract and confusing, because the young child hasn't accumulated enough life experiences and associative skills to put all those pieces together, even with a time line. In the early years I recommend that you just do a general overview of American history with your kids.

Nothing exhaustive, but just enough so that when Aunt Susie says something about the Pilgrims at Thanksgiving, your children don't say, "Who?" It just doesn't look good, and it causes your relatives to start questioning whether you should be home schooling your children. At this stage, you are simply going to snuggle up with your children and read to them a lot, but the books you choose will cover everything children of that age need to know about American history. No one will expect them to know much about world history at that age, but they will be expected to know about George Washington, and the Pilgrims, and Abraham Lincoln, and so forth. Let me share with you some key authors who will help you study American history during the early years until you are ready to jump into a time line.

Perhaps my favorite authors are a husband and wife team, Ingri and Edgar D'Aulaire. Ingri was from Norway and Edgar was from France and Italy. They met in Munich in art school, fell in love, got married, and moved to America. They have written a series of the

---

**HISTORY IS THE LOGICAL CORE OF
ALL THE REST OF THE CURRICULUM.**

---

most unashamedly conservative and patriotic biographies of famous Americans you could ever find. Each book also reflects a strong Judeo-Christian influence. For example, they share about George Washington's mother praying with him each night and Leif the Lucky becoming a Christian and bringing Christianity back to his people. They also tell the real story of Pocahontas, who was actually the first non-white convert in the New World, was baptized, and changed her name to Rebecca. Our children have been robbed of these truths about famous Americans that the D'Aulaire books still contain.

Every child needs to read the D'Aulaire books. There are several of them currently in print with titles like *Leif the Lucky, Christopher Columbus, Pocahontas, George Washington, Benjamin Franklin, Abraham Lincoln, Buffalo Bill* and *The Star Spangled Banner.* The illustrations are beautiful because the D'Aulaires were artists, and there is a full page illustration on every other page. So raise your children knowing and loving each and every one of these books.

Keep in mind that any time you can use a biography to teach history, you should do it. Children have no interest in dates and treaties. They want to know about the people who lived long ago, and they really want to know about children. What did they wear? What were they like? Were they naughty? Did they home school too? All of the D'Aulaire books start by sharing events in the childhoods of these famous people.

Biographies are a wonderful "hook" into history, because once children care about the famous person, then they want to know about wars, treaties, dates, kings and queens, and so on. Once a child has an interest in a famous person, then the child will want to know what was going on in the time at which that person lived. Education in a nutshell is studying the people of history.

You need to hang out in the biography section of your library, because many of the most wonderful books are out of print. Get a library card and teach your children how to find what they need in the biography section. But when selecting biographies, always remember that older is better. If a book was written in the 1950s or earlier, you will probably like it. If written in the 60s, it will be "iffy." In the 70s you're on your own, and in the 80s and 90s, don't waste your time. This isn't to say that there are no good books written nowadays, but if you're new at this, just stick to the older books until you build your confidence. Once you know the difference between a good book and a bad one, you can find the good ones in any time period.

Here are some other great authors for the early years:

1. **Marguerite de Angeli**. She wrote *Door in the Wall*, *Thee Hannah*, and a number of other wonderful books, many of which are now out of print.

2. **Alice Dalgliesh** is best known for *The Courage of Sarah Nobel*, but has written many other great books.

3. **Laura Ingalls Wilder** wrote the *Little House on the Prairie* books. Every child needs to read these books at least twice while they are growing up. These books are "Homeschool in a Box," because you can build a whole year's worth of study around them by getting *The Little House Cookbook*, *The Laura Ingalls Wilder Songbook* and *The Prairie Primer* (a unit study course which follows all the Wilder books).

4. **James Daugherty** wrote many fine biographies that are great "read-alouds" for this age group.

5. **Margaret Pumphrey** wrote a little book called *Stories of the Pilgrims*. This is an absolute treasure of a book that will tell your children things about the Pilgrims they will never find anywhere else.

RECOMMENDATIONS FOR THIRD GRADE AND UP

At around third or fourth grade children are usually reading fairly well, so now is the time to start looking into ancient history. Your two tools for working with third graders and up are time-lines and unit studies. A time-line doesn't have to be anything fancy. You can buy ready-made blank ones or you can just get some shelf paper or butcher paper, mark it off into sections according to what you are going to be studying with centuries or groups of centuries, put the dates in for your children and even do the writing in of the names and events. This way they only have to do the illustration part, which is the fun part to them.

If your children are not creative or artistic, there is no reason they can't draw stick figures or cut up magazines or even an old set of encyclopedias from a garage sale. But they need to do their own illustrations and not buy something ready-made. This way they have a sense of "ownership" in the creation of the time-line.

I've been asked, how do we choose what to put on the time-line? Well, you divide it into manageable sections of years based on what you are studying at the time. You don't want it to be overwhelming. The key word is "representative." What events represent, or sum up, what we want to remember about a particular time period?

Now, let's spend some time discussing the theory behind a unit study. I'm sure most of you have heard the term "unit study." There are many different definitions and expectations for what a unit study should be. When I was new to home schooling, we tried various prepared unit study programs that we purchased. I felt very locked in and intimidated and not in my niche. As I became more seasoned at home schooling, I realized how easy it is for anyone to develop a unit study on their own for free using only a Bible and a library card.

History gives a logical progression to build a unit study around. After all, you are not going to keep reading about Ancient Egypt forever, you must move on to Greece, and Rome, the Middle Ages, the Renaissance and Reformation, Modern Times, and American History. So using history as your framework keeps you moving.

The concept of a unit study is studying many different subjects, at many different levels, around a common core theme. What if you have four children and each child has six or seven subjects to cover? Who could teach four grades of seven subjects at the same time? Not even Superwoman could do it. It's not realistic unless you put each child in front of a TV and feed in educational videos all day. I was a trained teacher with a graduate degree and only expected to teach one subject each day in public school, and I could hardly keep up with that!

When using a unit study approach, the whole family is studying the same thing at the same time, only at different levels. The younger children may be reading picture books about Ancient Egypt while the older children are reading independently something quite demanding, but they are all covering the same information and studying within the same focus, which is Ancient Egypt.

Where prepared unit studies and I parted was when I was a young home schooling mother. I was supposed to gather all this stuff, stay up nights preparing all the information and materials, then get up the next morning and spit it all back to my child as some sort of "all-knowing one," then stay up the whole next night and start the cycle all over again. For me, that lasted for about three days, then the unit study program went in the closet.

That's not what I want you to do. All I want you to do is read out loud with your children, learning with them as you go. Most of us, de-

---

HISTORY GIVES A LOGICAL PROGRESSION
TO BUILD A UNIT STUDY AROUND.

---

pending on how much education we have had, know very little about the history of Western civilization. I knew practically nothing. When I became a Christian, I attended a church in California and whenever the pastor would use a historical analogy, like comparing someone in the Bible to Peter the Great, I didn't have a clue who Peter the Great was. I was part of the Baby Boom generation. I went to the best East Coast schools and we never studied history or read a piece of classical literature. Instead we read authors like J. D. Salinger and Kurt Vonnegut and e e cummings. Heaven forbid if we ever read something like *The Scarlet Letter*!

One of the beauties of home schooling is that you get to fill in your own educational gaps. If you never studied a particular era of history before, you get to do it now with your children. But it's not a matter of staying up nights and cramming in a lot of information you never knew before so you can teach it to your kids. That is not what I want you to do. I want you to get up with your children in the morning and read your Bible and then sit and read together for an hour or two. Do some math, then go outside and play or garden or dig ditches, or come back inside and bake and cook. Just live real life. My point is that you are learning with your children as you go by reading good books together.

What books do you need? First there are source books. These are books you are going to use for every unit that you teach. My desire would be that you take three or four years to get through a study of history from ancient times to the present, so these source books will constantly be there as resources for you to refer to.

The first source book I recommend is *How Should We Then Live?* by Francis Schaeffer. Everyone needs to own this book. Francis Schaeffer was a leading Christian theologian who wrote this book as a treatise on the rise and fall of Western culture. Chapter by chapter he covers the history, culture, and worldview of different eras from early Rome through the Age of Reason—all from a Judeo-Christian perspective. So he tells you about the artists, painters, sculptors, musicians, and philosophers as well as historical figures, focusing on their worldviews and what was the over-riding premise of the culture they lived in. To my mind, this book is the base of teaching a child how to think Christianly. When our son was growing up, I said, "J.J., if you can master *How Should We Then Live?* and the multiplication tables, I will be a happy camper."

The corresponding book to HSWTL was written by Jane Stuart Smith and Betty Carlson, two women who were Schaeffer's associates. Both women were musicians, and they wrote a book called *The Gift of Music*, which is a history of music starting with King David and moving forward in time through several hundred composers in chronological order. So if you have a child who has any gifting or interest in the realm of music, this is the history of music from a Christian perspective. It is amazing to read this book and discover how many of the early composers were believers. For example, Bach wrote at the beginning of every piece, "To the Glory of God," and he signed each piece with "By the Grace of God."

These are things we were never taught in school. It's such a joy to learn them now with your children. Other resources you will be turning to again and again are *Men of Science, Men of God* (biographies of famous scientists), *Streams of Civilization, Volumes 1 and 2* (history of the world from a Christian perspective) and *Kingfisher History Encyclopedia.* Also, *A Child's History of the World* by A. V. Hillyer is a great book if you ignore the first four or five chapters. These are all books you will keep zeroing in on through the years.

Another book that makes my heart sing is by Os Guinness. He and his friend Dr. Louise Cowan, who is a professor in Texas, have compiled *An Invitation to the Classics*, subtitled "A Guide to the Books You Always Wanted to Read." What they have done is prepared a history of literature by presenting, in chronological order, important literature in the history of Western civilization.

They start with Homer, move through the Greek poets, the Romans, the Middle Ages, and so on to the twentieth century. Each chapter analyzes each author's work from a Christian perspective, explaining his or her worldview, and summarizing the plot of some of his or her writings. Some of the authors were Christians and others were definitely not, and your children need to know which are which. This isn't to say you must never read an author who isn't a Christian, but you want your children to know where the person they are reading is coming from so they can be discerning. You don't have to agree with everyone you read, but you do have to be exposed to these different great minds for the purpose of criticism and analysis.

An Invitation to the Classics is junior high and high school in a book.

Not only does it provide a framework of literature to read as you study different historical periods, but it is such a help to know what the different authors believed, so you can study worldviews at the same time.

HOW DO WE BEGIN?

Now that we have some understanding of what we plan to do, how do we begin? The obvious answer is that you will begin at Genesis, chapter 1, verse 1. Read the Bible, and maybe Ruth Beechick's *Adam and His Kin* until you get to Joseph being sold into Egypt. Then you are going to study Ancient Egypt, then Ancient Greece, then Rome, and so on, moving forward through history, using the Bible and good historical literature.

Egypt is not a super-important historical period as far as a contribution to Western civilization is concerned, but the contribution of Ancient Greece is gigantic. If you had to spend a whole year studying Ancient Greece, it would be time well spent. Greek thought is foundational to all of Western Civilization and is also foundational to the history of Rome. Once you get to the study of Rome, you will find that the Romans didn't have an original thought in their heads! Everything Roman was really Greek, so you will see the time you spent studying Greece was very well spent. Also, the New Testament was written in Greek because at that time Greek was an international language, much as English is today. The Apostle Paul had a classical Greek education, being raised in Tarsus, and he also had a classical Hebrew education, being trained under Gamaliel. The New Testament, particularly the Book of Acts, is going to come alive for you as you study Ancient Greece and Rome. You are going to see Paul and Christ quoting classical Greek writers. That went over my head for years because I had never studied these things before. For example, when Jesus spoke of wolves in sheep's clothing, he was quoting Aesop, a Greek slave, and when Paul said, "Bad communications corrupt good morals," he was quoting a classical Greek writer. You see, if we don't study the classical writings, we don't realize how much involvement there is of the classics in the New Testament.

I also want to expose you to a very important piece of Western literature, probably the most important work of classical literature, and that is *The Iliad* by Homer. Homer was a blind Greek who brought together many of the oral traditions of the story of the Trojan War and wrote them down in the form of an epic poem. Rosemary Sutcliff, a modern British author, wrote a narrative version of *The Iliad* and also of *The Odyssey* (which is the story of the travels of Ulysses). *Black Ships Before Troy* is exquisitely illustrated and made appropriate for children. When you read it you will understand why it has become a modern classic. It is a great story that parents tell me their children read over and over again. And best of all, it's a boy's book. It's hard to find good books for boys, but this is one that will grab your boys.

The question always arises, "What about mythology? Why do Christian children need to know about myths?" I will agree that it may not be wise to expose young children to mythology, because they have a hard time distinguishing between fantasy and reality. But once a child reaches the age where he knows the difference and has an understanding of truth, Greek mythology becomes no different from any fictional story.

The reason everyone needs to at least be exposed to Greek and Roman mythology (and even some Norse) is that it is alluded to in every piece of classical literature your children will ever read. Mythology has also become a part of the speech of everyday life. For example, they may hear someone say, "He just opened a Pandora's box," or "That was her Achilles heel," or "She has a face that could launch a thousand ships." Understanding the myth behind these analogies is knowledge that all well-educated people share in common, and it is part of a body of knowledge that people will expect your children to own if they want to operate in a literate society. People who have been robbed of familiarity of these things, as I was, go through life like they are seeing with only one eye. When I was a child and read Louisa May Alcott's *Little Women* and *Little Men* and all her allusions to Greek myths, I had no idea what she was talking about. So please give your children this part of a classical education to equip them to function in the realm of great literature.

Now I am going to discuss another author everyone must read. Most of you don't realize that you are living in the Golden Age of Home Schooling and that many books you can get easily were not available to people who home schooled ten or fifteen years ago. I would have to go through dozens of out of print book searches and spend hundreds of dollars to get the same books you now buy from home school suppliers for $15.00 each. One of the authors I used to move heaven and earth to find books by is Genevieve Foster. She lived in Illinois in the 1930s and 40s and was deeply concerned about the lack of good historical literature for her children to read. So she decided to write books herself. I think she is the very finest history author for children of all time.

The first book Genevieve Foster wrote was *George Washington's World*. She then went on to write books about the world at the time of Columbus, John Smith, Abraham Lincoln, Augustus Caesar, and many other famous historical figures. Her books are so magnificent because she takes a famous person and covers his lifetime, using that person as a springboard to tell what was going on all over the world during that slice of history. The books give you an international view of history during a specific time period. The concept is terrific, but what really makes Genevieve Foster great is that she is a great writer.

Before her death she said, "When I write, I craft every sentence as if it were a precious jewel." So her books don't read like history textbooks, but like great literature.

What you are looking for in teaching history is books that make your child want to stay up late reading them under the covers with a flashlight. Your kids will be begging to read these books, so don't spoil it by telling them they will be "learning history" by reading them. Genevieve Foster's books are irresistible, because she makes you know and understand the people she writes about. With Genevieve Foster's books you can cover from Ancient Rome forward, and most of American history. Her *Augustus Caesar's World* is the perfect core book for a study of Ancient Rome.

After Rome, you will move to the Middle Ages, which is every little boy's favorite period. Boys would be happy to stay in the Middle Ages until they graduated from high school. There are many great books about knights, particularly the Arthur series by Rosemary Sutcliff, and *A Boy's King Arthur* by Sidney Lanier.

After the Middle Ages, go to the Renaissance and Reformation. This is when you will introduce your children to Shakespeare. Years ago in England there was a writer named Charles Lamb who had a sister named Mary. They were both gifted, brilliant people, concerned that the children of England were not becoming acquainted with the works of Shakespeare. So the Lambs decided to retell Shakespeare's plays in a narrative form easily understood by children. Their book *Tales from Shakespeare* has become a classic and is the perfect introduction to Shakespeare for children. When you read it with your children, start with the comedies, like "Taming of the Shrew." Read it. Act it out. Go to a play. Stick to the comedies first, then move on to the tragedies and you will discover why Shakespeare is called "the Bard of the Bible" because his work is so biblically based in the Judeo-Christian ethics of right and wrong and sowing and reaping. You will also discover why he is the best-selling playwright of all time. But don't tell your children, "Oh, this is hard!" or "Oh, this is good for you!." Just read the plays and let your children fall in love with Shakespeare as countless people have done before them.

From the Renaissance and Reformation, you can move on to modern world history, and finally reach American history after you've built an understanding of the history of Western Civilization. When you study American history, your core resources will be the series by Peter Marshall and David Manuel: *The Light and the Glory, From Sea to Shining Sea*, and *Sounding Forth the Trumpet*. Read these in the original versions, not the children's versions, for the Christian backdrop to events from Columbus to the last century.

Three other resources will help you find books that are appropriate for each time period and age level. The first is *Honey for a Child's Heart* by Gladys Hunt. The second is *Books Children Love* by Elizabeth Wilson. And the third is *Turning Back the Pages of Time* by Kathy Keller, which only deals with American history. All three provide booklists by historical period and age group, but each takes a little different approach and lists books that the others don't, so it is best to have them all.

This chapter was written by Carole Joy Seid. Carole homeschooled her son, J.J. using a study of history and reading good literature as the basis of her curriculum. She is a popular homeschool conference speaker. Most of the books Carole recommends can be found at the Home School Marketplace website.

19

TEACHING SCIENCE AT HOME

SCIENCE OFTEN INTIMIDATES PARENTS who want to teach creatively. There are several reasons for this. First, modern science has become so highly specialized, each branch with its own vocabulary, techniques, paraphernalia, and "ivory tower" mentality, that we think it is beyond the understanding of the average person. Cold fusion experiments and quantum theory are the stuff of which government grants are made, not concepts that seem relevant to everyday life.

The second major reason science seems difficult is that modern man is out of touch with the natural world. We no longer interact with plants, animals, or the environment in ways that allow us to learn and apply scientific principles. What former generations knew about animals because they kept livestock or about the weather because they spent a lot of time outdoors we now have to learn from books. What once was a natural part of life has become very unnatural and even forced.

The third reason for dreading science is that most science teaching materials are laboratory oriented and information intensive. Things are taken out of their natural setting and studied in parts, laboring over details and bits and pieces. All of the information is "second-hand," because the student never interacts with the real plant, animal, or whatever in its natural setting. Even the physical science experiments tend to stress entertainment or acquisition of bits of information.

How can science be made interesting, creative, and less intimidating? We believe that there are seven foundational principles involved in teaching science in the home school.

Principle 1 | Recognize that the natural world tells us about God. Suppose someone asked you, "How can I know what God is like?" What would you say? The Bible tells us three ways God has revealed Himself. The first two ways are through His Word: His written word (the Bible) and His Living Word (the life of Jesus reflected in Christians). The third revelation of God is found in the created world: "For since the creation of the world His invisible attributes, His eternal power and divine nature, have been clearly seen, being understood through what has been made...." (Romans 1: 20). The apostle Paul, who wrote this verse, assumed nature's revelation of God is so clear that those who ignore it are "without excuse." Furthermore, those who fail to notice God in creation tend to engage in all sorts of sin.

This is why Creation Science is so important. Without a Creator, there is no need for a Savior. The major areas of scientific study are built upon the contributions of men who believed that the world was created by a reasonable, orderly God Who placed certain laws within His creation. Francis Bacon developed the scientific method; Carolus Linneaus began biological classification; Johann Kepler founded physical astronomy; Robert Boyle began the modern study of chemistry; and Isaac Newton laid the foundations of physics and developed calculus into a comprehensive branch of mathematics. "Living within the concept that the world was created by a reasonable God, scientists could move with confidence, expecting to be able to find out about the world by observation and experimentation" (Francis Schaeffer in

175

How Shall We Then Live?). We too can be confident that whatever we study in science can teach us what God is like.

Principle 2 | Nurture a sense of wonder. The poet Gerard Manly Hopkins wrote: "The world is charged with the grandeur of God!" Small children innately understand this. They are quick to marvel, to "oooh" and "aaah" over an interesting cloud formation, a pile of autumn leaves, a puddle filled with tadpoles, a variegated rock, a wriggly newborn kitten. Sadly, as they grow older, children have such

---

MODERN MAN IS OUT OF TOUCH WITH THE NATURAL WORLD. WE NO LONGER INTERACT WITH PLANTS, ANIMALS, OR THE ENVIRONMENT IN WAYS THAT ALLOW US TO LEARN AND APPLY SCIENTIFIC PRINCIPLES.

---

hectic schedules, so many man-made experiences, and so much electronic stimulation that they often have to be trained to appreciate nature. We feel that science as science should come after the development of a sense of wonder about nature. Preschool and elementary aged children should explore, observe, collect, and marvel at the natural world without parents being teachy about it.

Principle 3 | Develop naturalists first, then scientists. Scientists take things out of their natural setting and study their parts, teaching details, dissecting and analyzing. This fragmenting of something alive and fascinating can strip it of its allure. In contrast, the naturalist studies plants, animals, and rocks out in nature. He appreciates the uniqueness of each created thing, learning its habits, its patterns, its interaction with other created things. He develops a sense of wonder about nature. Many of the parables Jesus told were addressed to people who understood the patterns of living things, of the seasons, and of the weather. We've lost those understandings because we no longer interact with the natural world on a daily basis. Helping our children become naturalists will restore understandings of the attributes of God that creation can teach us.

Principle 4 | Create a context for learning to occur in the most natural way. Find good books about animals or about people and animals (not textbooks, but interesting stories). Subscribe to a nature magazine for children. Invest in field guides. Maximize your opportunities to interact with nature through nature walks, field trips to nature centers, camping, having pets and spending a lot of time outdoors. Let children cook, fool around with magnets and compasses, wire a light socket, move loads using simple machines, etc.

Principle 5 | Don't expect your children to be what you or they are not. Don't try to make them who they are not. If your great love and talent lies in music, chances are your children will be more musically inclined than scientifically inclined. Conversely, some kids just do not like spiders, snakes, hikes, and so forth. Don't force these things on them.

Principle 6 | Focus on wisdom and knowledge, not on information. What do our children really need to know? Science curricula are developed to fill one hour a day, 180 days a year. Even if a concept takes only 5 minutes to communicate, a textbook has to devote a classroom session to it. Not only is there a glut of information, but the information tends to be "predigested," telling the child what it all means and what he or she is to think about it. This is what we call "informational overkill." We have to be realistic about our children's needs. Do they show a real bent towards science or nature study? If so, our teaching can be more in-depth in those areas. If not, we need only cover essential concepts and knowledge. A very helpful book for determining the necessary science skills is *What Your Child Needs to Know When*. It lists science concepts the institutionally educated child might be taught at each grade level through eighth grade. You will find that many of these concepts can be communicated just by reading books, taking nature walks, and letting your children help around the yard and the kitchen.

Principle 7 | Be open to God's lessons. We don't have to search for spiritual meaning in what we teach. If we are seeking the Holy Spirit's direction, God will create opportunities to use whatever we are studying to bring us closer to Him. I'll give you a personal example involving tadpoles. One day several years ago when our family was experiencing severe financial difficulty I took a walk in a pasture near our home. Our financial pressures were weighing heavily on my mind, but I noticed that the pasture was dotted with small puddles of water and each puddle was teaming with frog eggs or tadpoles in various stages of development. There were millions of potential frogs in that one pasture, but I knew that most of the puddles would dry up before the tadpoles could fully mature. I began to think what a waste it was for God to create all those little lives only to have them die, and I asked, "Why did you do this? You knew these tadpoles wouldn't have a chance of survival!" Even as I was asking I began to understand that what I was seeing was the lavishness of God, the "exceeding abundance" that Scripture speaks of concerning Him. A line from a hymn came into my mind: "His grace has no measure, His love has no limit,

His power has no boundaries known unto man; for out of His infinite riches in Jesus He giveth, and giveth, and giveth again." At that moment I knew God would be sufficient for all of our needs. Now every time I see a tadpole I am reminded of this lesson.

AN OVERVIEW OF SCIENCE STUDY

Exactly what is science? Science is the study of God-created things and systems. There are four major branches of science study:

Life Science is the study of living things. The big concepts in Life Science are (1) the characteristics of being alive (eat, grow, reproduce, respond, basic unit is the cell); (2) taxonomy (the organization of living things into categories based on their similarities and differences); (3) vocabulary or nomenclature (most scientific words are derived from Latin or Greek); and (4) understanding of systems (like photosynthesis, respiration, digestion, the food chain, etc.).

Earth Science is the study of non-living phenomena. The big concepts in Earth Sciences are (1) a general understanding of the major branches: Meteorology (study of weather); Astronomy (study of stars, planets, and outer space); Geology (study of rocks and minerals, the makeup of the earth); (2) understanding of earth-related processes and systems (the water cycle, how rocks are formed, the dynamics of weather systems, etc.)

Physical Science is the study of heat, sound, light, electricity, magnetism, gravity, energy, work systems, atoms and molecules, states of matter, and chemical reactions. Physical Sciences would include Physics (heat, light, sound, electricity, magnetism, gravity, energy, work systems), Engineering (application of principles of physics), and Chemistry (study of atoms and molecules, states of matter, chemical reactions).

Social Science is the study of man and his interaction with society. Social Science would include Sociology (man's interaction with man, cultures, etc.); Anthropology (how man lives and his social systems); and Psychology (mind and emotions and how they affect human behavior).

VOCABULARY AND NOMENCLATURE

Learning scientific vocabulary is like learning a foreign language. In fact, since most science words are derived from Latin or Greek, science vocabulary is a foreign language! Many of the terms have to be learned strictly as vocabulary words in the course of studying various scientific concepts, but it is very helpful to use a program that teaches the most common Latin and Greek roots. Programs like *Vocabulary Vine, Living Roots, English from the Roots Up* or *Rummy Roots* give children a head start on scientific vocabulary and make words like photosynthesis easily recognizable. For example, in Greek, "photo" means light, "syn" means together, and "thesis" means to put or set in order). So, the word, "Photo-syn-thesis" means the process plants use to take in sunlight and combine the light with other elements to create their own source of nourishment, or food.

SCIENCE IN THE LOWER GRADES: NURTURING A SENSE OF WONDER

Most young children have a natural love of nature and the outdoors and a natural interest in magnets, electricity, and machines. Our job in the elementary years is to nurture that love and provide children with opportunities to explore the world around them.

If you look at what is actually taught in the elementary grades in science, you will realize that most of what children are expected to know can be learned in the course of exploring their environment. We believe that science in the elementary grades should consist primarily of:

1. *Nomenclature*: Learning the names of things like types of cells, parts of a cell, types of plants, parts of a plant, parts of the body, major taxonomic groupings (major classes of living things), types of envi-

ronments, stars and planets, rocks and minerals, chemical elements, physical properties (like osmosis, mass, evaporation, refraction).

2. *Observation and collection:* Collecting and studying rocks, insects, feathers, leaves, flowers, and so on.

3. *Identification:* Identifying the most common plants, animals, rocks and minerals, constellations, and weather patterns.

4. *Experimentation:* Fooling around with magnets, circuits, rockets, chemistry sets, engines, and interesting experiments that develop the child's natural interest in physical science.

5. *Understanding systems:* Developing a general understanding of processes and systems like the food chain, the water cycle, various body systems (digestive, respiratory, circulatory, etc.), ecosystems, and more.

6. *Wondering:* Nurturing what naturalist Rachel Carson called "a sense of wonder" about the natural world.

TIPS FOR TEACHING SCIENCE TO ELEMENTARY AND MIDDLE GRADES

1 | Read lots of books about animals. An annotated list of good literature about animals can be found on the Home School Marketplace website. Subscribe to a nature magazine. *Ranger Rick* is for elementaries and is published by The National Wildlife Federation. It occasionally mentions evolution and is definitely conservationalist in tone, but is filled with interesting stories about animals and lots of wonderful full color photos. *Nature Friend Magazine* is a Christian counterpart to *Ranger Rick.* For older students, *Smithsonian, National Geographic* and *National Wildlife* focus on nature study. Most states have wildlife magazines that feature plants, animals, and scenic wildlife areas of that state. Also, don't forget that there are excellent nature videos available. The National Geographic's *Planet Earth* videos are outstanding.

2 | Collect the tools of the trade. This includes field guides, binoculars, magnifying glasses, an insect net, pinning board and pins, a plant press, an aquarium with wire mesh lid, magnets, a quality compass, and as finances allow, a microscope.

3 | Invest in field guides. Sure, you can check them out of the library, but children live in the now and you lose the critical nurture point for interest if you postpone studying the critter until you can get the field guide from the library. Start with the field guides in areas of greatest interest and in areas you are most likely to study—usually birds, insects, trees, reptiles and amphibians, stars, weather. We prefer the *Audubon Pocket Guides* for beginners because they have pho-

---

MOST YOUNG CHILDREN HAVE A NATURAL LOVE OF NATURE AND THE OUTDOORS AND A NATURAL INTEREST IN MAGNETS, ELECTRICITY, AND MACHINES. OUR JOB IN THE ELEMENTARY YEARS IS TO NURTURE THAT LOVE AND PROVIDE CHILDREN WITH OPPORTUNITIES TO EXPLORE THE WORLD AROUND THEM.

---

tographs, their compact size is appealing to children, and they cover only those animals, plants, or minerals children are likely to see. For more advanced study, we like the big, comprehensive *Audubon Society Field Guides*.

4 | Expect short attention spans. Since it is hard for children to be quiet and still, start by studying created things that can't run away—rocks, flowers, trees, stars, clouds and weather. Insects are also easy to study because they are so abundant. Progress to animals that require patience and quiet in order to study them in their natural habitats—like birds, reptiles, amphibians, and mammals.

5 | Teach taxonomy. Even young children can learn that there are five types, or Kingdoms, of living things (plants, animals, fungi, bacteria, and protists) and that each of these Kingdoms is made up of different kinds of organisms. This doesn't have to be formally taught, but can be communicated when you are walking ("Look at that! Some trees lose their leaves in winter and some don't. Trees that lose their leaves are called deciduous, trees that don't are called evergreens. Ferns are plants too, but they are different from trees. Have you noticed ways they are alike? Ways they are different?")

6 | Make your own field guides. Since our children were very young we have kept an index card box to catalog their "finds." Whenever one of the boys brought home a critter, we would look it up in a field guide and write out its common name, its classification, and its scientific name. For example, the card on a box turtle reads: "Box Turtle, *Terrapene carolina*. Kingdom: Animalia, Phylum: Chordata (has a spinal cord), Subphylum: Vertebrata (has a backbone), Class: Reptilia (cold-blooded, with scaly skin), Order: Chelonia (has shell and horny beak), Family: Emydidae (pond and river turtles), Genus: Terrapene (pond turtle with movable hinge on lower shell)." After doing this a short while, the boys clearly understood the major taxonomic groupings. We also have traced, cut out, or photocopied the pictures from field guide coloring books and then colored them to make our own field guides. (It is permissible to photocopy the drawings for personal use if you have purchased the book.)

7 | Take frequent nature walks. Agree on rules beforehand, like hand signals instead of talking, what the children are to look for, what they are not allowed to do. Don't expect much the first several walks, but after awhile you will notice your children becoming more observant, patient, and quiet.

8 | Involve all of the senses. Invest in audiotapes of bird songs, frog calls, and night sounds. Learn to recognize signs that animals have been about through their tracks, scat, or markings. Hear things, smell things, touch things, even taste things.

9 | Keep a pet in a jar. Some critters make good pets. Consult a field guide as to which ones are better kept in captivity. Habitats can be as simple as a large glass jar and as elaborate as a landscaped terrarium. The book *Pets in a Jar* has instructions for collection and care of many small wild animals.

10 | Start a nature journal. This may be as simple or as detailed as you like. It can focus just on trees or on birds or can cover as many life forms as you choose. It can be a combination diary, picture album, field notebook, or whatever you wish. Two excellent examples of nature journals are *The Country Diary of an Edwardian Lady* and *A Naturalist's Notebook*.

11 | Keep a garden. A garden allows you to effortlessly teach many aspects of plant study. If there's not room for a vegetable garden, try a small patch of flowers. Consider choosing varieties that attract butterflies and hummingbirds or that have medicinal value.

12 | Breed animals. Allowing your child to have a pet will open many doors into understanding the natural world. If you can breed an animal (dogs, cats, fish, gerbils or cows, horses, goats, etc.) sex education, genetics, and most areas of anatomy and biology become "real world" learning so that they are more interesting and, therefore, more easily learned.

13 | Feed whatever interests develop. For example, if the child becomes interested in rockets, let him concentrate on building rockets for as long as he is interested. (Watch the movie *October Sky* to see where kids fooling around with rockets can lead.) Ditto radio controlled planes, electronics, telescopes, leaf collecting, or whatever. Help provide raw materials, literature, and anything else that will support the interest for as long as it lasts.

Although teaching science to your children may seem like an overwhelming task, what needs to be known in the elementary grades can easily be taught through activities such as observing, collecting, categorizing, and identifying common animals, plants, rocks, and fungi; keeping a nature journal; and reading interesting books together about animals, plants, scientists, and life processes.

Some of the most appealing books for elementary and junior high ages are the Usborne books.

SCIENCE IN THE UPPER GRADES

High school is the time to assess what the future holds for our children and to determine how in-depth or serious their study of science should be. Use the elementary grades to study plants, animals, minerals, heat, sound, light, electricity, magnetism, and machines firsthand and spend as much time outdoors as possible. Save the laboratory and serious study for high school.

By eighth or ninth grade you should know your child's scientific inclination. If he or she shows a natural bent towards science or plans a career requiring a great deal of science, high school is the time for more serious study and independent research projects, possibly in conjunction with a local continuing education program.

If a lot of science is not in your child's future, find out your state's (or the future college's) "bare minimum" science requirements and focus on covering those skills and concepts.

TIPS FOR HIGH SCHOOL SCIENCE STUDY

1 | Be sensitive to what your children's desires really mean. A child may repeatedly express a desire to become a doctor, or nurse, or veterinarian, engineer, or another profession requiring a lot of science. Examine these desires closely. We know a child who has wanted to be a veterinarian ever since he was very young. So, of course, the parents arranged for the child to help at a veterinarian's office, to visit the Veterinary School's open houses, and to spend time doing things related to becoming a veterinarian. After a long period of "feeding the interest," the parents realized that this child doesn't really want to become a veterinarian. He loves horses and thought if he became a veterinarian he would be able to spend a lot of time with horses. Sometimes children express a desire for a certain career because of a misconception of what that career will involve or because that is the

> **HIGH SCHOOL IS THE TIME TO ASSESS WHAT THE FUTURE HOLDS FOR OUR CHILDREN AND TO DETERMINE HOW IN DEPTH OR SERIOUS THEIR STUDY OF SCIENCE SHOULD BE.**

only profession they have ever heard of that includes some of what they would like to do.

2 | Continue feeding whatever interests have developed. Research into the critical factors in the lives of people who are outstanding in their fields versus people who are not particularly successful shows that it takes approximately 10,000 hours (or 10 years) to really master something, whether that something is a musical instrument, a sport, or computer programming. So if your child shows a particular interest in something, feed the interest and give him or her the time and resources to accumulate 10,000 hours following that interest. Read the book *Outliers* by Malcolm Gladwell for stories of children who were allowed to invest 10,000 hours in their interests and what that led to in their lives.

3 | Find help for your weak areas. If you feel insecure teaching high school science, find people willing to either tutor your child or help you over the rough spots. Our former church was filled with retired scientists from the atomic energy laboratories at Oak Ridge, TN. Sometimes they helped one-on-one and other times they taught groups of home schoolers once a week, giving assignments to be done at home. Another option for parents who find science instruction intimidating is to rent the video science courses from Abeka or School of Tomorrow.

4 | Don't worry about leaving "gaps." Fear of leaving educational "gaps" is what usually drives parents of teenagers to prepackaged curricula or scares them into sending their children to public school. However, most states only require two high school science courses for graduation, and the requirements usually don't specify exactly which sciences have to be taken. This means that no matter what your child takes, there will be gaps.

If he takes earth science and biology, there will be chemistry and physics gaps. If he takes biology and chemistry, there will be earth science and physics gaps. Unless your child takes every science course imaginable in high school, there will be gaps. So feel free to forget about gaps and focus on those science courses you think will be most helpful to your child.

Usually the best two science courses to cover in high school are Biology and Chemistry. If you are worried about whether your child will score well enough on the ACT or SAT to be accepted by a college, invest in some guides to these tests and find out exactly the science concepts covered. Another idea is to buy a guide to the Advanced Placement Test in Biology (or the CLEP test in Biology) and gear your high school biology course to the test. That way your child may be able to do well on the AP or CLEP test and exempt college biology courses.

5 | Don't be intimidated by lab sciences. Another fear in the hearts of teaching parents is that they will have to teach labs in biology, chemistry, physics, and who knows what else. This is not true. Generally only one of the sciences required for high school graduation is a lab science. If there are no restrictions in your state as to what that lab science must be, you can substitute many things for lab science. For example, study electronics and have the child wire a lamp, a shed, or a room addition. If you have a microscope, study microbiology.

For Botany lab, collect, press, and catalog plants. Plastic models of humans or animals can take the place of dissecting, or you can purchase dissecting kits to accompany anatomy study. There is even an on-line virtual frog dissection.

The Everyday Science Sourcebook suggests experiments using common materials for any scientific concept you happen to study. Other good labs would be to help a veterinarian or a midwife for a semester, or take a CPR or First Aid course. Since the whole point of laboratory study is to reinforce the scientific concepts being learned and to allow the student to participate in the Scientific Method and learn to record data in a scientific way, you can devise your own labs to accomplish these purposes.

6 | Give the child more responsibility. We once attended a homeschool conference where, during a question and answer session, a man shared his frustration with a teenaged son who hated school. All the boy seemed to want to do is fool around in his father's workshop. David Colfax, the main speaker, told the parent to consider having his son build a room addition to the house. We were astounded at this answer, but saw the great wisdom in it. If the boy really did build a room addition, he would learn math, electronics, building skills, thinking skills, financial skills, and who knows what else, plus he would have acquired valuable building experience. The high school years can be a time for practical application of many scientific concepts, such as keeping a garden, raising livestock, building and wiring a storage building, and so on.

TEACHING SCIENCE USING THE SEASONS OF THE YEAR

Whatever the age, if you want more "real-life" application of science, it is helpful to plan studies around the seasons of the year.

Spring and summer are the best times of year for plant and insect study. Animals can be studied year around, but spring is a better time to visit zoos and farms because you may be able to watch babies being born. Winter and spring are the best seasons for bird study because in winter you can attract birds to a feeder more easily and most bird song occurs in the spring. Winter is also the best time for astronomy because the night skies are clearer and there is less haze in the air than other times of the year. Don't even bother to look for reptiles and amphibians in the winter. The best seasons for studies of these creatures are the spring and summer. Ecology is best studied outside, so plan on hikes and time spent outside when the weather is mild.

Save inside study topics for winter. These would be dissection projects, microbiology, and cellular biology, and any other science study that requires time spent inside or a lot of book work. Almost any science textbook can be adapted to a "seasonal" schedule. You just have to scan the text and schedule the times of year you would like to study each portion.

For lists of the best science books for studying all the different science subject areas, go to www.homeschoolmarketplace.com.

20

THE IMPORTANCE OF NATURE STUDY

WHY IS IT IMPORTANT TO STUDY NATURE? Many of us have lived so long in urban environments that not only are we out of touch with nature, but we are suspicious of attempts to get back in touch with nature, thinking them New Age.

We've also been so conditioned by our Western worldview to think of nature as a commodity that we no longer see ourselves as part of the natural world. Our Greek academic heritage has made us "observers of," not "participators in" what God has created. We feel more comfortable bringing a plant into a laboratory, dissecting it, and "mastering" its fragments than we do taking a nature walk and getting to know plants as plants.

The Sioux Indians believe that animals and plants talked before the white man arrived. Maybe animals and plants still talk and we just have lost the ability to listen. The Bible certainly assumes that the natural world has a lot to say to us. Scripture gives us two reasons why nature study is important:

1 | Observing and understanding nature is one of the ways man can know about God. Romans 1 tells us that God's invisible attributes and divine nature can be clearly seen through what He has made. Psalms tells us that the heavens "declare" and created things "speak" about the glory and wonder of God.

2 | Contemplating nature instructs and inspires God's people. Many spiritual truths are explained using examples from nature. Some Scriptures are John 15 (vine and branches); John 10 (shepherd and sheep); Romans 11 (being grafted into a tree); John 12 (a grain of wheat); Matthew 17 (faith as small as a mustard seed); and Matthew 6 (God's care and provision for wildflowers and birds). Jesus often used natural examples to explain the Kingdom of God and He assumed that His hearers were familiar enough with the natural world to understand His examples. Many Biblical writers used plants and animals for moral instruction. (Example: A lazy person was directed to watch the ant and imitate her industriousness.)

Once we know the importance of studying nature, we don't want to just use creation as fodder for Bible studies or character development. This approach is as fragmenting as laboratory dissection and just as manipulative as seeing created things as commodities. We need a holistic view of nature that includes understanding, appreciation, wonder, and wise stewardship, as well as application in Bible studies.

About Evolution

Unfortunately, many outstanding books on nature reflect an evolutionary view of the origin of life, promote an "old earth" theory, or contain elements of native American religions. We have chosen to recommend a few books with references to evolution or Indian methods because we cannot find anything their equal in teaching value, quality of illustrations, or ability to promote interest. When we use these books, we turn the non-Christian statements into opportunities to teach our children that we live in a fallen world and fallen man has come up with false ideas about how everything got here. We refer to Romans 1 which states that God has made Himself clearly known through creation and that people who refuse to acknowledge the Creator suppress the truth about reality. Our children can recognize subtle as well as overt references to evolution, and understand that what a person believes about creation affects how a person lives.

We also tell them that people without a Creator feel no need for a Savior. As Ruth Beechick says, "This is the message our society needs today. After people believe in a Creator God, we can talk to them

---

WHY IS IT IMPORTANT TO STUDY NATURE? MANY OF US HAVE LIVED SO LONG IN URBAN ENVIRONMENTS THAT NOT ONLY ARE WE OUT OF TOUCH WITH NATURE, BUT WE ARE SUSPICIOUS OF ATTEMPTS TO GET BACK IN TOUCH WITH NATURE, THINKING THEM NEW AGE.

---

about the Savior. If people are in that evolutionary life chain with no purpose but what they create for themselves, what place is in their thinking for something like the cross? None at all; it is only foolishness. People first need the preaching of the Creator God." The best creationism books we've found are *Unlocking the Mysteries of Creation* and *It Couldn't Just Happen*.

NATURE WALKS

"Nature walks" are the best way to become familiar with the natural world. For those of you to whom this is an alien concept, here are some suggestions and explanations.

192

Taking a nature walk simply means you are going to place yourself and your children in the context of living, breathing plants and animals. You are going to interact with them first-hand rather than through books or in a laboratory.

You don't have to have a National Park handy to take a nature walk. This can be done in your backyard, in your city park, or in a neighbor's field. If your city has a nature center, there will often be a pre-designed nature trail you can walk. However, the trails at nature centers are usually so overused that there is little left to see.

If at all possible, find an area that has both open spaces and woods and is near water. Animals have three basic needs—food, water, and shelter—so if you can find an area with all three, you are more likely to see a variety of wildlife.

1 | Prepare beforehand. Find books about the different plants and animals in your area and have some idea of what you will look for. It is better for the children if the first few nature walks actually turn up something interesting, so plan the walk in an area and at a time when the wildlife you want to see will be observable. For example, pick a few common birds, a few common plants, and a few common insects that you are almost guaranteed to see and make them the object of your first few walks. You can prepare the children beforehand with sheets to color (from *Field Guide Coloring Books*), with bird songs to listen to, and with field guides to look at.

An inspiring book to read beforehand (you can even read aloud to your children) is *Naming Nature*. The author set out to make the acquaintance of her natural neighborhood and realized that if she learned just the most common plants, birds, and animals around her, she would probably recognize most of what she saw. So she learned one name at a time, a few names a week, for a year. *Naming Nature* chronicles her year of naming things and is a wonderful guide for amateur naturalists.

Other very helpful books are *The Field Guides to Wildlife Habitats*. These are the only books that take you habitat-by-habitat (sandy beach, lake and pond, swamp, etc.) and tell you what to look for and listen for, and how to find both plants and animals in each different habitat. With these guides you can take a nature walk anyplace in the United States.

If you live in the city, *Peterson's First Guide to Urban Wildlife* is very helpful because it covers all the creatures a city child is likely to see.

2 | Make it enjoyable. If you and your children are not used to spending a lot of time outdoors, you must prepare beforehand so that it will be a pleasant experience. Pick a time of day when the temperature is comfortable and no one is tired or hungry. Wear the proper shoes and clothes; put on insect repellent and sunscreen; perhaps take drinks and a snack. Start with short excursions of 30 to 60 minutes. The times can be lengthened as interest builds.

Your boys will love it if you make the whole nature walk into a military-type "recon mission" to spot certain plants and wildlife before returning to "base."

3 | Invest in the tools of the trade. As finances allow, begin acquiring the following: A pair of lightweight binoculars for each person, a hand lens, a few pocket field guides, stout walking sticks for probing in holes and under rocks and logs, a small field notebook, and something to hold treasures your children may find. If you want to encourage your children to keep a nature journal, have the supplies on hand: a blank journal, pens, colored pencils or markers, etc.

4 | Agree beforehand on the behavior you expect. Nothing is more frustrating than having a unique "nature moment" spoiled by a loud "Hey! Look at that!" Agree beforehand on the behavior you expect: no loud noises, no running ahead or hanging behind, no damage to the landscape, etc. It is also helpful to develop military-type hand signals for "Gather around," "Look at that," "Go this way," "Stop here," and other frequent communication you may have during your walks.

Make sure the children understand basic safety rules such as never sticking their hands into a hole or brush pile without first probing with a stick, never entering water without your permission, and so forth.

Also be sure they can recognize any poisonous plants (particularly poison ivy), snakes, or insects they might encounter.

5 | Gradually increase the level of difficulty. As children become used to nature walks, you can demand longer periods of silent attention, you can take more lengthy excursions, you can go out in uncomfortable weather, etc. A wonderful book that begins with simple observation techniques and gradually introduces advanced observation, tracking, and survival skills is *Tom Brown's Field Guide to Nature Observation and Tracking for Children.*

DIFFERENT FACETS OF NATURE STUDY
Plant Study

Plants are the easiest form of wildlife to study because they stay put. We suggest that you start with the trees, shrubs, and flowers nearest you and learn something about them before taking walks through the forest. Try learning just a few plants a week, finding out their names and something about them.

Invest in the *Familiar Trees* and *Familiar Flowers* books of the Audubon Pocket Guide series and the *Trees* and *Wildflowers* books of the Audubon First Guide series.

Just by studying these four books and identifying the trees and flowers your children see, you will be able to cover much more than the basic knowledge of plants grades K - 8 require. Plant study is best done in the spring and fall, but the book, *Nature in Winter*, tells you how to identify trees in winter by their bark, shape, and buds.

Leaves and flowers are easy to press in layers of cardboard and newspaper sandwiched between two pieces of 1/4" plywood held together by bungee cords. After allowing them to dry in the press for two weeks, the leaves or flowers can be mounted on heavy paper. Position them on the paper with small dots of glue, then cover them with clear Contact paper or slip the papers into plastic sleevees. Each page can include information about the plant, and can be kept in a notebook. If your children are keeping a nature journal, pressed leaves and flowers can easily be mounted on the journal pages.

Another wonderful way to study plants is to have a garden. If space is limited, even a window box of flowers will do.

Children love flowers, and enjoy having their own plot of ground to plant whatever they want. Children are particularly fascinated with plants that attract butterflies or hummingbirds and plants with medicinal value.

Insect Study

Insects are best studied in the warmer months, unless you live in a temperate climate. Tools of the trade are (1) an insect net (easily made from an old minnow net, simply replace the fish netting with muslin for catching insects or bridal-type netting for catching butterflies and moths); (2) a kill jar (a plastic or Mason jar with a lid and about half an inch of plaster of Paris poured in the bottom); (3) a magnifying glass; and (4) an insect field guide. If you intend to start an insect collection you will also need a pinning board and pins. The pinning board may be home-made from balsa wood (from a hobby shop) and hat pins will do, but it is better to buy some insect pins and a board made specifically for the purpose of mounting insects from a biological supply house or homeschooling catalog.

If you are just beginning your study of insects, start with a simple collection device, such as the *Insect Collector's Kit* and *Creepy Crawlies Kid Kit*. A good book that takes you through insect study step-by-step is *The Insect Almanac*.

If you can only afford a few books on insects, buy the big *Audubon Society Field Guide to Insects and Spiders*, the *Audubon Society Field Guide to Butterflies*, and *The Insect Almanac*.

These three books will give you a foundational knowledge of insects as well as tips on collecting, pinning, and mounting them. Children love to collect and with a little help are able to create really nice collections that can be displayed.

Insects can be caught in many different ways:

1. "Sweeping." Walk through a grassy field, brushing the net back and forth across the grass in a sweeping motion. Empty out the net into your kill jar or examining jar.

2. "Beating the bushes." Place an old white sheet under trees or bushes. Shake the bushes and pick up insects that drop to the sheet below.

3. Turn over rocks and logs to find beetles, ants, termites, grubs, etc.

4. Butterflies and other flying insects can be netted. If you make the net part of your insect net long enough, you can net a butterfly and then flick the end of the net over to keep the insect inside. However, be aware that some butterflies and moths are considered endangered, so it is better to just capture them, examine them and then release them.

5. Moths can be attracted to porch lights at night and then netted. Another way to attract moths is to paint a sweet syrup mixture on trees in your yard, then collect the moths that come to it at night. Once you have captured an insect, you can either examine it alive or place it in a kill jar for a few minutes and then examine it dead. Activate the kill jar by soaking a little fingernail polish remover (containing ethyl acetate) into the plaster of Paris.

Reptiles and Amphibians

Reptiles and amphicians are much harder to spot than birds and insects, and this makes their firsthand study more challenging. It's futile
to search for them in the winter unless you live in a temperate climate.
Here are some tips for finding reptiles and amphibians:

1. *Make a list of the reptiles and amphibians found in your area.* This list
can be derived from field guides, but often your local wildlife agencies
will have lists, literature, or even posters of the reptiles and amphibians

---

"NATURE WALKS" ARE THE
BEST WAY TO BECOME FAMILIAR
WITH THE NATURAL WORLD.

---

you can expect to find. It is very important that you and your children can recognize the poisonous snakes in your area. Study pictures
of them; make up mnemonic devices for remembering them such as
"When red touches yellow, don't touch the fellow!" (coral snake); and
learn warning signs like if you smell cucumbers in the woods it means
a copperhead is near. Teach children to probe with a stick, not with
hands, and to wear boots in snake infested terrain.

2. *Finding Amphibians.* Except for the breeding season, when salamanders search for mating sites and frogs and toads call to prospective
mates, amphibians are rarely seen or heard. Many amphibians are
nocturnal and can be found in numbers only during late winter or
spring rains. Frogs are best found on warm spring nights near water.
Only male frogs call, and during early spring they may call both day
and night. Once you hear calls coming from a puddle, pond, or even
a neighbor's swimming pool, you can usually approach carefully and
capture both males and females.

Toads can also be found in moist areas around the foundations of buildings and in gardens. Caution!!! Toads do not cause warts, but they do secrete an irritating substance. Make children wash their hands thoroughly after handling toads. Salamanders can be found in the daytime by overturning large rocks in creeks or streams or by carefully lifting wet leaf debris.

3. Finding Reptiles. Reptiles will venture out later in the spring then do amphibians. Reptiles "bask" to raise their body temperature, so can be seen sunning themselves on spring and fall afternoons or in early morning or late afternoon in summer. When summer temperatures rise, reptiles may become nocturnal.

Water turtles can be found basking on logs or rocks near water; snakes also have favorite "sunning" rocks, and lizards can be found on the sunny sides of fence posts or buildings. Be sure to look under flat rocks, pieces of bark, logs, leaf litter, or in stump holes or tunnels. Piles of debris as well as abandoned farm buildings are ideal reptile hiding places. Never try and catch a snake with your bare hands! Immobilize the snake's head with a forked stick or by placing your booted foot over it, then grasp just behind the head so that the snake cannot turn and bite you! You can make a snake and lizard snare by attaching a fishing line noose to the end of a bamboo pole, so they can be caught from a safe distance.

4. Keep a pet in a jar. Many reptiles and amphibians make good pets. Consult a field guide and the book *Pets in A Jar* as to which ones are better kept in captivity.

Bird Study

Birds are easy to study because they are found almost anywhere at all seasons of the year and don't require much stealth and quiet to observe. Birds will come to feeders year-round, but the best time for feeder projects (except for hummingbirds) is in the winter.

Birds sing when they are nesting (spring and early summer), usually in the morning and early evening, so spring mornings are the best times to listen for birdsongs and late winter is the best time for bird house projects. Fall is the least productive time for bird study unless you live in a migratory pathway.

The basic tools of the trade for studying birds are: a decent pair of easy-focusing binoculars (preferably 7 x 35 or 8 x 40); a field guide, such as the *Audubon Pocket Guide to Familiar Backyard Birds*; and a CD of bird calls. Once you have these, you can begin doing the following:

1. Contact your local nature center, ornithological society, and/or wildlife resources agency. They will have lists of birds found in your area, often by frequency of occurrence. The library may have a "birders' guide" to your state. These agencies may also have free literature about birds or even movies. For example, the Tennessee Ornithological Society has a convenient checklist of all the birds found in Tennessee, so we make a contest of seeing who can check off the most birds on the list.

2. Armed with a list, begin looking for birds first in your backyard, then as you go on nature walks, and so on.

3. Make or buy bird feeders for your yard. Put bird feeders where you can watch the birds eat. Birds will even come to your window if you put a feeder there. Most birds that come to feeders will eat black oil sunflower seed. You can buy it in bulk at garden supply centers. Don't waste your money on commercial birdseed mixes because they contain a large percentage of seeds that only attract the less interesting birds. Be sure to put up a hummingbird feeder in the summer and plant red, nectar producing flowers.

4. Begin learning the birds one at a time. We have had great success making our own field guides by cutting out or copying pictures of birds we see from the *Field Guide to the Birds Coloring Book* and allowing the children to color each bird while listening to a tape of its calls. Soon the boys were able to identify many birds by their songs.

5. *Put up bird houses.* This is a good way to learn nesting preferences. *Building for Birds* is an excellent guide to building birdhouses. The major groups of birds that will use bird houses are bluebirds, chickadees, wrens, titmice, sparrows, and starlings. Starlings are considered very undesirable, so be sure the bird houses you buy or make have the right sized entrance holes to exclude them. Birds who do not nest in houses (such as robins) will sometimes nest on small platforms attached to the side of a building.

6. *Participate in bird counts.* When your children are beyond the beginner bird-watching stage, arrange with your local ornithological society to go along on their spring and fall bird counts.

Studying Seashores, Ponds and Streams

Children love water—splashing in it, fishing in it, catching all kinds of creatures in it. No science study is complete without visits to ponds, streams, and the seashore.

Study of ponds and streams and seashores is best done in the late spring, summer, and early fall, except in temperate climates. Some favorite books are *Ponds and Streams*, *The Edge of the Sea*, *The Seaside Naturalist*, and the Audubon Pocket Guides to *Familiar Seashells* and *Familiar Seashore Creatures*.

Mammals

Unless you live on a farm or in a more natural area, your ability to study mammals in their natural habitats will be limited and even on nature walks you are likely to see only the most common rural and urban animals—squirrels, chipmunks, and perhaps raccoons, opossums, and mice or rats. But it is not difficult to arrange a visit to a farm or to the zoo and take your "nature walks" there, studying the farm or zoo animals.

You also can have pets. Dogs, cats, gerbils and hamsters all can become subjects of your study of mammals. We've also found veterinarians to be very agreeable to letting home schoolers tour their facilities and even observe surgery. And if you have a veterinary school near you, these often have "open houses" where you can get a behind the scenes tour of the whole school.

Stars and Planets

Unless you live in an area with low light pollution at night, you will have a hard time studying astronomy. But there's no reason you can't take drives out into the country to study the night sky or visit a planetarium or even purchase one of those devices that projects the night sky on the ceiling, like the *Star-gazer Planetarium.*

Children of all ages are fascinated with telescopes, binoculars and star-gazing and a good pair of binoculars is essential to all forms of nature study. Our favorite binoculars are by Bushnell because they are reasonably priced and their optics are very good.

Our favorite star-gazing book for beginners is A. H. Rey's *Find the Constellations.* This book delights children with its interesting illustrations and fascinating stories about the stars and constellations and teaches them to read the night sky.

For a more in-depth, advanced study of the night sky, choose *40 Nights to Knowing the Sky* which could be used as a semester in astronomy because it leads you step by step through the fundamentals of astronomy in literally 40 nights. Nights 1 – 30 only require "naked eye" viewing, but nights 31 – 40 require a telescope or binoculars. We also love the book, *Astronomy for All Ages.*

KEEPING A NATURE JOURNAL

Rather than teaching science from a textbook, why not let each child keep a nature journal?

The Country Diary of an Edwardian Lady is a wonderful example of how nature, art, literature, and history can be interwoven. In 1906 Edith Holden began a nature journal in which she recorded and illustrated what she saw month by month during walks in the English countryside. She began each month's entry with historical events associated with that month and listed major holidays with brief historical explanations. The rest of each month's entry consisted of notes of what she saw on her frequent walks interspersed with drawings of selective wildlife and plants. She also included poems and famous quotations about the month or about the things she saw. Her watercolor illustrations are exquisite and her Victorian penmanship is a delight to read.

Another great example is *The Naturalist's Notebook*. It is a nature journal in photograph form.

There's no reason children could not follow a similar format. If drawing is a problem, buy several of the field guide coloring books and let the children trace and then color illustrations for their journals. Flowers, leaves, and grasses can also be pressed and then mounted to the journal pages with clear Contact paper.

Classification and detailed study of certain topics, such as the parts of a flower, can be included. Such an approach can incorporate history, nature study, art, weather study, literature, penmanship, and whatever else you can imagine, even personal entries and photographs. It can be done for as long or as short a period of time as you like.

If a year seems intimidating, try it for a month, particularly in the spring, summer, or autumn, or during a family trip.

OUR FAVORITE NATURE STUDY AND SCIENCE RESOURCES

1 | Keeping a Nature Journal by Clare Walker & Charles Roth. This is the nature journaling "how-to" book we have been wishing for. It explains the equipment you will need, gives simple and encouraging sketching lessons, tips on different ways to develop a nature journal, plus ideas for journaling in each season of the year and many pages with samples of journaling styles. A beautifully done, very special book that will make you long to start your own nature journal.

RATHER THAN TEACHING SCIENCE FROM A TEXTBOOK, WHY NOT LET EACH CHILD KEEP A NATURE JOURNAL?

---

2 | Field Guide Coloring Books. Based on Peterson's field guides, these coloring books picture many of the most common animals and plants individually or in woodland, desert, backyard, countryside, mountain, and swamp habitats to color. We have cut, photocopied, or traced portions to illustrate nature journals. (It is permissible to copy the pictures for your own use.)

3 | Reader's Digest Guide to North American Wildlife covers the most common plants, animals, insects, and sea life in North America and is an invaluable reference book.

4 | Audubon Society Field Guides are the BIG, comprehensive field guides (5" x 8" x 1½" thick) with flexi-vinyl covers. You should buy as many as your budget allows, because you will use these all through the home schooling years and beyond. We like these better than the

Peterson's guides because they have photographs rather than drawings.

5 | *Audubon Society Pocket Guides.* We like pocket guides best for ages 8 and under because they have color photographs instead of drawings, their compact size (4" x 6") appeals to children, and they cover only things a child is likely to see. Each guide is about 200 pages with each left side page a color photograph and each right side page a brief description of the animal and its habits and habitat.

6 | *Peterson First Guides.* These are the only non-Audubon guides we recommend, because they cover areas of animal life not found in the Audubon pocket guides. *Peterson's First Guide to Urban Wildlife* covers the city wild creatures a child is likely to see. *Peterson's First Guide to Caterpillars* shows caterpillars, their coccoons, and the moths or butterflies they become.

7 | *National Audubon Society Regional Field Guides.* The animals, plants, and natural environments of different regions of the United States are fully described in these nifty field guides. Each guide contains more than 1,000 accounts of local animal and plant species; clear explanations of each region's natural history, climate, and night sky; information on all the best parks, preserves, forest, and sanctuaries; and nearly 1,500 color illustrations, photographs, maps, diagrams, and drawings. These are wonderful alternatives to buying separate field guides for birds, trees, wildflowers, night sky, etc.

8 | *National Audubon Society First Field Guides.* Absolutely stunning guides for elementaries, with the most beautiful photos you will ever see. Each guide has four parts. For example, in the Amphibians guide, the parts are: (1) "The World of Amphibians" which gives lots

of interesting information; (2) "How to Look at Amphibians" tells you what you need to know to begin identifying them; (3) "The Field Guide" includes detailed descriptions, range maps, and photographs of the 50 most common North American amphibians; and (4) "The Reference Section."

9 | *Find the Constellations* delights fourth through eighth graders with its interesting illustrations and fascinating stories about the stars and constellations and is a book to be used year around, indoors and out.

10 | *Tom Brown's Field Guides* are written by the famous Tom Brown, who is America's foremost authority on tracking and wilderness survival. His books mention Apache Indian beliefs, but there are no others that give such in-depth information about tracking and wilderness survival. *Tom Brown's Field Guide to Nature and Survival for Children* covers learning to observe the natural world, identifying animals and plants, lost-proofing, and ways to survive in the wild. *Tom Brown's Field Guide to Nature Observation and Tracking* shows you how to move as silently as an Indian, how to spot and identify animal tracks and signs, and more.

11 | *Pets in A Jar*. How to find, catch, and keep many small animals such as butterflies and moths, earthworms, water bugs, hydras, toads, newts, pond snails, crickets, tadpoles, praying mantids, and more. For ages 9 and up and extremely useful to mothers whose children keep bringing home "critters." If you intend to study animals in a hands-on way, this is the book to have.

12 | *The Weather Wizard's Cloud Book*. We have used this book over and over for the past few years. The author explains that today's clouds

tell you tomorrow's weather, and he provides page after page of color photographs of the sky showing different types of clouds and how to interpret the kind of weather each predicts.

13 | *A Handbook of Nature Study* by Anna Comstock. A huge book (887 pages) originally published in 1911 that gives lesson plans and background information on every aspect of nature study. Major divisions are Animals, Plants, Earth, and Sky. This book is the closest we've found to Charlotte Mason's suggestions for nature study. The lesson plans assume you can actually go outside and look at or work with the subject at hand. For example, the section on birds has you teach using a live chicken, because everybody in 1911 had chickens handy. (Even a parakeet will do.) Great resource for the land-based, a challenging opportunity for city dwellers. All ages.

14 | *Tracking and the Art of Seeing* by Paul Rezendes. "Our encounter with nature is largely a matter of seeing, and it relates to the quality of attention in our lives." With full color pictures, the author not only teaches animal tracks, signs, and habits, but also teaches how to be attentive to what animal signs are telling you.

15 | *Nature in Winter* by Donald & Lillian Stokes. Winter can be just as rich a time for nature study as the other seasons. In-depth guide (over 400 pages) of things to look for and do in winter. It covers plants, animals, weather, and more. For parents with elementary ages, or middle schoolers up to use alone.

16 | *Sciencescope* by Kathryn Stout. A unique book that explains how to teach science and what to teach from first grade through high school. Includes all the skills, topics, and concepts a child is supposed

to learn and how to teach them plus what to expect from different ages. Great resource for planning multi-age unit studies.

17 | *Mysteries and Marvels of Nature*. A lavishly illustrated, exciting, hardcover Usborne book written in a "Ripley's Believe It or Not" style. Teaching Home Magazine's "Pick of the Crop" for best science resource. Contains Mysteries and Marvels of Plant, Animal, Reptile, Bird, Ocean and Insect Life. Boys love this book.

18 | *The Usborne Illustrated Encyclopedia of the Natural World* provides a wonderful overview of the natural world—plants, animals, classification, and ecology—with gorgeous illustrations and interesting text. There are detailed diagrams and cut-aways explaining scientific principles as well as activities, projects, and habitat maps. Ages 9 up.

19 | *The Everyday Science Sourcebook*. An unusual compilation of every conceivable experiment you can do to demonstrate any science concept you happen to be studying. All experiments use easily found materials. All ages.

20 | *Great Science Adventures* by Dinah Zike and Susan Simpson are the best science studies out there for zeroing in on a particular area like plants or vertebrates or birds for grades K - 8. Each different book has 24 lessons that thoroughly cover all that age group needs to learn about the particular area of science study in wonderful, hands-on ways. Teacher pages include vocabulary words, concept maps, assessments, assignments for all grade levels, and enrichment activities. This is a super resource that kids will love using, especially boys.

21 | *Boy Scouts of America*. The Boy Scouts offer merit badges in

many areas of science and nature (Botany, Reptiles and Amphibians, Birds, Wilderness Survival, Astronomy, etc.). There is an inexpensive booklet for each merit badge. These booklets are packed with information and wonderful project ideas and each booklet could form the basis of a semester's study of a particular scientific area. Contact the BSA Council office.

22 | 4-H Clubs. Contact your local Agricultural Extension Service about the different 4-H activities available in your area. We have found 4-H to be very open to home schoolers forming their own clubs. Project booklets are free and are available in dozens of science areas such as entomology, forestry (focusing on trees found in your state), wildlife, livestock, etc. The project books are arranged by grade levels, starting at 4th grade, and contain lots of ideas for science study. Our 4-H allows us to have the project booklets even if we are not enrolled in a particular project.

23 | Wildlife Resources Agencies. Your state probably has an agency dedicated to preserving wildlife. These agencies can help you with free literature (even nature film rentals) and give you addresses of other state and federal organizations that have nature resources.

All of the books mentioned in this chapter plus many more nature study resources are available at www.homeschoolmarketplace.com. There is also a downloadable e-book available on **Teaching Science at Home** *that goes into greater depth about science study in the home school.*

POSTSCRIPT

CONGRATULATIONS! You are now ready to find the teaching materials you need that support the relationships, life skills, and information in your course of study for each child.

If you've followed along in our two books, *I Saw the Angel in the Marble* and *I Carved the Angel from the Marble*, you now understand the philosophies and educational approaches influencing the different home schooling materials, you know your children's learning styles, you know your own educational philosophy, and you know what academics, practical skills, and relational skills are important for you to cover with your child in each school year. Now you can start assembling the products and resources that are congruent with your family's values and priorities. You can find many of those products and resources at the Home School Marketplace website.

Prepare to spend several hundred dollars and maybe a few months getting clear about what you want to do. If it makes you feel any better about the amount of time and money you have to spend getting ready to teach your children, think of it this way: The average public school teacher has spent four to six years and more than sixty thousand dollars learning how to teach your children in a classroom. Why shouldn't you spend some time and money preparing yourself to teach your own children at home?

However, and this is a BIG however, don't think that you have to have everything figured out before you begin. You can adapt as you go. So loosen up and accept the fact that some of what you try will be a total waste of time, energy and money. This is all a part of learning what works for you and for your children. Consider it payment of your tuition as a parent in Home Educating U.

So, just relax and have fun with home schooling!

RESOURCES

ABOUT THE RESOURCES WE RECOMMEND.... We don't recommend everything available to home schoolers for two reasons—first, because no matter how good they may be, most of the resources marketed to home educators are either unnecessary or patterned after public school materials, and second, because we've limited our advice and selections to materials we have used with our own children or to items friends we trust rave about that are educationally sound. That way we can stand behind each product and say, "It works!"

We're aware of a lot of educational junk food out there that does nothing to nourish young minds and hearts. We are also aware that home education has become an industry and many people with no interest in or experience with homeschooling are beginning to cash in on this market. We believe homeschooling is part of a move of God to restore the family, and we don't want to merchandise what God is doing, we want to service it.

HOMESCHOOLMARKETPLACE.COM WEBSITE

The great Irish poet William Butler Yeats once said, "Education is not the filling of a bucket, but the lighting of a fire." Whether you are just considering home schooling or a seasoned veteran at it, we've developed products that will help you "light a fire" in your children's hearts and minds instead of treat them like "buckets" to be filled with academic information.

First, there is *I Saw the Angel in the Marble*, the prequel to the book you are now reading. This first book focuses on the foundational aspects of home schooling—the attitudes, thinking, and environment that allow you to set your children free to become the individuals God created them to be. Then there is *I Carved the Angel From the Marble* which focuses on the nuts and bolts of educating children at home.

Next, we are developing a series of unconventional guides to home schooling that cover each of the topics introduced in *I Saw the Angel in the Marble* and *I Carved the Angel From the Marble* in more detail.

As you look over our guides, they are meant to help you through a progression of changes in your heart and your head about what education is; about who your children really are; about what their real needs are and how you can meet those needs; about how your children learn best; about how to identify your family's unique meaning and purpose; about how to choose the best teaching materials for your situation; and about how to prepare your children for a future that may be as radically different from our adulthood as ours was from our parents and grandparents.

These unconventional guides to home schooling cover four tracks, or themes: (1) understanding your child and his/her educational needs; (2) teaching methods and materials; (3) different approaches to education; and (4) putting it all together in such a way that it encourages a lifestyle of learning. We also have guides that cover different facets of home life and home business.

Each guide is around 50 pages long and thoroughly covers one topic in easily readable form. Think of the guides as highly digestible "meals" that will nourish your spirit, mind, and soul throughout your home schooling journey. All of the guides can be purchased at our website: www.homeschoolmarketplace.com.

Here's just a sampling of the guides we offer and are in the process of developing:

- The first guide, *A Strong Enough Why* leads you into developing such a strong conviction about why you are home schooling that you can weather any storm and the "Hows" will take care of themselves.

- When asked how he could carve such beautiful sculptures, Michaelangelo is said to have replied, "I saw the angel in the marble and carved until I set him free." The guide *Seeing the Angel in the Marble*, gives you the knowledge and tools to identify who each child really is, in spite of the fact that sometimes you feel like you're looking at a "block of marble."

- *See How They Grow* gives you a deeper understanding of the mental, emotional, and moral stages a child goes through from birth to age 18 so that you will be able to home school each child in an age-appropriate way.

- *Helping Them to "Get It"* gives you tools to identify the ways each of your children learns best.

- The two guides *What's Out There* and *Home Schooling in Freedom* explain the different teaching materials and approaches available to home schoolers and walk you through the process of creating your own scope and sequence that is tailored to your family's needs.

- *Creating a Family Mission Statement* helps you discover your family's goals, values, uniqueness, meaning and purpose and walks you through creating a Family Mission Statement that can become a guide to the way your family operates in every area of life, including home schooling.

- Once you've discovered the heart of your children and of your family, the next several guides lead you through the process of discovering your educational philosophy, charting a course for each child, understanding the common educational approaches in home schooling, and choosing your teaching materials. They give you tools and understandings to craft your own individualized educational program for each child in each subject.

- *The Seven Habits of Highly Effective Home Schooling* explains the seven most important things you can do to ensure that your home schooling efforts are effective and successful.

- If you've ever suffered from a desire to throw up your hands and quit, the e-book *Home School Burnout* will help you stay the course.

- Sometimes when you are wearing all the different hats of home school Mom, wife, home-maker, chauffeur, and chief cook and bottle washer, life can get a little overwhelming. We have guides for that too—guides that will help you get off the "hamster wheel."

- We also have a series of guides on starting and building a family business.

You can find all of these guides and more, as well as the top resources in every area of home schooling at the Home School Marketplace website: www.homeschoolmarketplace.com.

EJOURNAL

Why not join us? The thousands of home educators who receive the Home School Marketplace EJournal get valuable and timely information about home schooling, home life, home business, and more delivered right to their email inbox. Through this online newsletter, we offer many new articles and thought-provoking essays through the

EJournal that we just can't fit into our books and guides.

Best of all, it's free. Go to www.homeschoolmarketplace.com and sign up for the EJournal. And, rest assured, we never sell, rent, or share our customer email list with anyone for any reason.

Go to www.homeschoolmarketplace.com and check it all out!

ABOUT THE AUTHOR

MOST OF THE CHAPTERS IN THIS BOOK first appeared as articles Ellyn Davis wrote for The Elijah Company catalog and its online newsletter. The Elijah Company was a family business begun by the Davis family.

Ellyn grew up in Atlanta, attended Georgia State and Emory Universities, earned a B.S. and M.S. and completed all but the dissertation for her Ph.D. in Microbiology/Biochemistry. After she married Chris Davis, they both became committed Christians. Ellyn has four children on earth and two in heaven.

Catrina, her eldest, is a social worker in Atlanta and has two children, Josh and Jake. Ellyn became interested in keeping her kids at home (instead of sending them to school) as she cried out to the Lord over problems she saw Catrina have in school. In 1981 a friend gave her Raymond Moore's book, *Home Grown Kids*, and a conviction about home schooling was deeply planted in her that has never wavered.

Her three boys have never known an institutionalized school setting. Seth, the oldest, graduated from home school, worked in the family business, and left home in 2001 to attend the Bethel School of Ministry in Redding, California. He has since served on staff at

Bethel Church, been an administrative assistant to one of the pastors at Morning Star Ministries, and eventually started his own website infrastructure and design company, *Curia Solutions*. He now lives in Redding, California. As Seth grew up he spent lots of time outdoors and soaked up anything having to do with nature. At 13 he was building and designing model rockets. At 14 he had developed a program for the Internet which was used all over the world. At 15 he was hired to assist the professor in teaching a computer science class at a local college. By the time Seth left home he had performed in numerous musical theater productions, was a decent pianist, a good basketball player, had taught himself several computer languages, was considered to be one of the premier young male tap dancers in the country, and had been offered a scholarship at a top university. Today, when he is not working or at church, you will find him hiking the Trinity Alps, snow-boarding, or hanging out with his friends.

James also graduated from home school, worked in the family business for awhile, then left home in 2001 to attend the Bethel School of Ministry with his brother. After leaving Bethel, he apprenticed for several years with a stock and options guru and learned to make a living on the stock market, taught dance, worked as a choreographer on several films and music videos, and started establishing his own entrepreneurial base. James began acting at age 10, and has worked professionally as an actor and dancer off and on since then. He still trades stocks and options and currently works as an entertainer for Carnival Cruise Lines and travels to different parts of the world. His great love is dance and he auditioned for the TV show "So You Think You Can Dance," winding up in the top 50 in a field of nearly a thousand dancers. James was also a champion horseback rider, winning both the State 4-H and Tennessee Quarter Horse Championships.

Blake opened in his first musical theater presentation at age 8. By

15 he was a professional actor and dancer. For years his passion has been the Middle Ages which he studies whenever he has a spare moment, which is not often. When Blake discovered a fear of heights, he became an ardent rock climber which he integrated into his Venture Crew Scouting experience on his way to becoming an Eagle Scout. Blake began his own photography business at age 17. His loves film and has worked on several motion pictures as an assistant producer, two of which have won independent film awards at major film festivals. Blake currently is following in his brothers' footsteps and attending Bethel School of Ministry while also pursuing his passion for film-making.

Ellyn started the Elijah Company in the late 1980s when she began home schooling the boys and found it impossible to find good teaching materials for them. Believe it or not, there was once a day when no one would sell curriculum to home schoolers, so whenever she discovered something she really liked she would buy a few copies for her friends. That penchant for finding good teaching materials for others eventually developed into a full-fledged business and Ellyn began speaking at home school conventions throughout the country as well as writing articles about home schooling that reached hundreds of thousands of families.

The Elijah Company became one of the largest home school supply companies in the world and not only supported the Davis family but several other families too until it closed in 2004. Since then, Ellyn has kept the spirit and the writings of The Elijah Company alive through a new business venture—Home School Marketplace.

CPSIA information can be obtained at www.ICGtesting.com
Printed in the USA
LVOW061913260612

287744LV00005B/97/P